A
Country
Naturalist's
Year

'There are some people who can live without wild things, and some who cannot. These essays are the delights and dilemmas of one who cannot.'

Aldo Leopold *A Sand County Almanac* (1948)

'He did not treat animals as pets, or as a pastime or a hobby. He turned to them for a renewal and enlargement of his being. His observations . . . spring from a participating recognition of the creatures' authenticity.'

Sylvia Townsend Warner *T.H. White* (1967)

'Never, ever miss the chance of a day on the hill. You'll always see something there that you never saw before.'

Gerard McMenamin, ghillie, Donegal 1980

A
Country
Naturalist's
Year
Colin McKelvie

ILLUSTRATED BY
Rodger McPhail

SWAN·HILL
PRESS

Other Books by Colin McKelvie

A Future for Game? (1985)
The Book of the Woodcock (1986)
The Woodcock: Studies in Words & Pictures (1988)
The Complete Book of Shooting (1988)
The Snipe: Studies in Words & Pictures (1989)
The Game Birds of the British Isles (1990)
A Gamefisher in Ireland (1991)
The Grouse: Studies in Words & Pictures (1991)
The Partridge: Studies in Words & Pictures (1993)

Edited by

The Roedeer (1987)
Wild Sports of the West (1987)
Wild Sports of the Highlands & Islands (1987)
South Country Trout Streams (1993)

Other Books by Rodger McPhail

Open Season (1986)
Fishing Season (1990)

Copyright © 1993 by Colin McKelvie (text)
Rodger McPhail (illustrations)

First published in the UK in 1993
by Swan Hill Press
an imprint of Airlife Publishing Ltd

British Cataloguing in Publication Data
A catalogue record for this book
is available from the British Library

ISBN 1 85310 446 9

Printed by Livesey Ltd., Shrewsbury

Swan Hill Press
an imprint of Airlife Publishing Ltd
101 Longden Road, Shrewsbury SY3 9EB

Contents

For Judy

with love

Preface

In this account of a country naturalist's experiences, I have ranged widely through notes and memories of the creatures and the places that I have encountered. In this I have not confined myself to the landscape and wildlife of Dumfriesshire, where I live, nor to Ireland, where I was born and grew up, nor to the Highlands of Scotland nor the chalk downlands of Wessex where I have lived and worked, and to which I often return. Instead I have included all these, and more besides, in what is a personal celebration of the wildlife and landscape of the length and breadth of the British Isles, throughout the seasons and in widely differing environments and habitats. In tracing these encounters with landscapes and wildlife, I have inevitably drawn upon the experiences and memories of several years.

It is one of the great delights of living in these islands that a day's journey, from Cornwall to Caithness, or from York to Cork, will take you through a variety of landscapes and a range of habitat types that are seldom encountered elsewhere within such easy reach of one another. By the standards of other countries and continents, the British Isles may be small and over-populated, but we still enjoy a natural variety that is worlds removed from the tedious sameness of endless prairies and steppes that may take days to cross, and that enjoys the daily uncertainty of variable weather, instead of the tiresome inevitability of predictable climates. The sea coast and woodlands and heather moorlands are all accessible within a few hours drive of any point on the face of these islands, and the geology, the vegetation and the animal and bird life change constantly as you drive, as also does the usually gentle but always capricious British weather.

I owe particular thanks to my friend Rodger McPhail, for the skill and sensitivity with which his watercolours have illustrated the text.

Colin McKelvie
Tundergarth House
Dumfriesshire
July 1993

The Water-Peggie

October signals the beginning of the noisy season for dippers. Or is this just an illusion, with the general autumn silence of most other birds making the dippers' calling seem unusually prominent? Not that these little birds are ever particularly quiet, as they whizz up and down the course of the rocky streams and the larger rivers with that quick, crisp, tri-syllabic *chip-chip-chip* that usually proclaims their presence long before you ever see them. But October means the start of their territorial claims, and the birds become especially conspicuous and chatty, flying incessantly as they patrol their chosen beats of the river, and calling a warning and a challenge to any others who might contest their tenancy. Never especially shy of man or dogs, they become even less wary than usual, perching alert on mid-stream stones until we are quite close and, once, actually flying around me in a tight turn and hovering momentarily above my rod point as I stood waist-deep in the river, casting in hopes of a late salmon. There is a certain comic daring in their behaviour at this time of the year, more than a touch of swagger and bravado as the tiny pert form struts and bows and bobs, and calls in high-toned defiance.

The dipper is such a distinctive character of the rivers and streams around my part of Dumfriesshire that my wife and I have adopted it as a sort of unofficial mascot, a bright little spirit that is almost certain to put in an appearance and enliven a visit to the riverside at any time of the year.

There are said to be five species of *Cinclus* dippers worldwide, three of them confined to Central and South America, and the western fringes of North America; one, the Brown Dipper, in east Asia and India; and the familiar Common Dipper of British and European rivers. It was not until I came to live in dipper country that I delved a bit deeper into the scientific literature and discovered just what a widespread and varied species it is. In Britain and Ireland it occurs almost everywhere among hilly and mountainous land, from the Highlands through south-western Scotland, north-eastern England, Wales and the West Country, and throughout the hills of Ireland. In the south of its Old World range it occurs in Scandinavia up to the Arctic Circle, throughout the mountains of North Africa, across Europe from Portugal and Spain to Poland and Bulgaria, and eastwards into the Urals and much of Turkey, Iran, Iraq, Lebanon and Syria, as far as southern Tibet and the western provinces of China. At the last count there were thought to be twelve distinct races or subspecies spread across this wide Eurasian range.

To tell them apart, live or dead examples of this little bird have to be minutely examined for tiny variations of marking and plumage coloration, and this is work more easily carried out by a ringer who takes the live bird out of the folds of his mist-net, or by the student studying preserved skins in a museum, than by a field observer with nothing more than binoculars or a telescope to help him. The benchmark example is *Cinclus cinclus cinclus*, the dipper of Scandinavia, France and Spain, while Great Britain has its own subspecies, *C.c. gularis,* and Ireland its very own *C.c. hibernicus*. Those who take the trouble to compare sample study skins and get an opportunity to handle live birds taken in ringers' nets can tell the difference between these three dippers of western Europe, mainly from the width of the reddish-brown border or narrow band of feathering that comes just beneath the dipper's smart white bib. This bright blaze is by far its most distinctive marking, at rest or in flight.

When I walk along the riverbanks near home in southern Scotland, or further afield in the Highlands, Ireland or Wales, the presence of dippers is usually first signalled by their song. That crisp, sharp call is penetrating and carries a long way, and once you know it, cannot be mistaken for anything else. Alerted by the sound, the eye scans the river's course for a sight of the bird, and it is usually the flash of that bright white bib that gives it away. A small black bird with a white breast might easily go unnoticed in a habitat of grey rocks and rushing white water, and we would probably miss a great many of them if they only stood still and merged into their surroundings. But there is a restless, fidgety quality about the dipper, which is forever bobbing and curtseying from its low perch on an isolated rock, or dashing like a black cricket ball equipped with fast, blurred wings, and always *chip-chip-chip*-ing to draw attention to itself. There is something in that repeated, sharp, one-toned, ringing call that must have reminded country people of the clinking and ringing of a hammer on an anvil in a smithy, and its names in Scots and Irish gaelic are *gobha uisge* — 'the water smith' — and *gobha dubh nan allt* — 'the blacksmith of the stream'.

But whether it is on the wing or just standing and bobbing, the dipper's bright white bib is always strikingly eyecatching, even on the dullest of winter days or in the half-light of dawn or dusk, and highlighted in contrast with the black and slatey-grey of the rest of its plumage. Its colour has given rise to a whole range of local and vernacular names. In much of Ireland and Scotland it is the 'water blackbird', which is a logical name, from the bird's blackness and the slight similarity of its song to the *pink-pink-pink*-ing of a cock blackbird, though perhaps a bit less accurate than the alternative 'water ouzel' or 'brook ouzel', which draw a comparison with the ring ouzel of the rocky hillsides, which also has a white bib. This black-and-white plumage is also reflected in other Scots and Irish names, including 'river pie', 'piet' and 'water piet', while the common country names from northern and western England — 'colley' and 'water colley' — concentrate more on the little bird's coal-blackness.

Its bobbing, curtseying movements are acknowledged in names like 'bobbie' and 'ducker'; and in Dumfriesshire I have also heard it called the 'water peggie', which I particularly like, since it seems to sum up the character and qualities of a little bird that is pert, alert, home-loving, jealous of its territory, and just a little bit fussy.

Dippers are so firmly wedded to their home stretches of stream, and so conspicuous in their calling and their flights, that they are among the easiest of all the birds of the upland fringes to watch. It comes as no surprise to discover that they are one of the most intensively studied of British birds, because they are easy to find, sedentary in their ways, and particularly easy to count, since they occupy the easily surveyed linear habitats of rivers and smaller streams. It might seem natural for a little bird of the open and often bleak hills and moorlands to forsake its usual surroundings for the gentler conditions of lower altitudes and milder, more sheltered areas in the worst of the winter. But the dippers hang on, even in the foulest and coldest of winters, because their preferred foods — the insect larvae and other invertebrates that live in shallow, well oxygenated streams

— are actually nearing their peak numbers in late winter and early spring. Many of these forms of underwater life are just waiting for the coming of warmer days and longer daylight hours to evolve into the next stages of their lives. A river on a warm June evening, with millions of insects hatching and fish rising and insectivorous birds feeding eagerly, may seem to be an infinitely more lively place than the same stretch of river on a bleak day in early March, but that is to overlook all the hidden richness that waits just out of sight under the water, poised to emerge into more obvious activity when the warmer days come. When the spring hatches of insects begin, the river is already beginning to lose some of that invertebrate richness that the dipper can exploit so skilfully by its special adaptation to feeding in and under the water.

Dippers feed in a way that is fascinating to watch, sometimes a little comic — and, when seen in close-up by the wizardry of modern filming techniques, quite unlike any other British bird. It does not feed simply by wading, like a heron or a snipe, or by diving in after some piece of prey, as a kingfisher does, but by immersing itself totally in the water, and then moving against the current by a combination of grappling with the rocks and gravel, and actually flying underwater, using its wings as angled vanes upon which the water pressure bears down to hold it in the current and in contact with the rocky stream bottom. Its diet may be a rich fare of protein in the form of insects, larvae and shrimps, but it is hard-won in strongly-flowing waters where the chill conditions and the bird's method of hunting combine to make severe demands on its energies.

The Leaper

No-one, it seems, is indifferent to hares. They have had a special grasp on the human imagination since the most ancient times, a fascination that mingles admiration with awe, delight and praise with uneasiness and a nameless fear. Often the hare is unmentionable, indescribable, 'unspeakable' in the biblical sense, something so special that its very identity cannot be disclosed in one bald straightforward word for fear of dreadful consequences. It must be sought and implied in obliquities and periphrasis, just as the adherents of some religions will shrink from the direct naming of their gods.

Among the treasures of the Bodleian library in Oxford there is a manuscript account of hares, in a style of handwriting that palaeographers ascribe to the late 1200s, and probably originating from the borders of Wales and Shropshire. That proximity to Gaeldom is probably significant. Here are no fewer than seventy-seven different names, each of them an indirect way of referring to the hare, 'the animal that all men scorn, the animal that no-one dare name'. In keeping with the Welsh poetic practice of the thirteenth century, this hare-hunter's prayer takes the form of a succession of descriptive epithets, to be first recited 'with sincere devotion' by him who would set out to hunt and take a hare. 'The starer with wide eyes', 'the looker to the side', 'the one who takes to the hills', 'the one who doesn't go straight home' — all are euphemisms for the hare; and around this shy little mammal has evolved a folklore as rich and neurotic as that of any creature, even the baleful wolf of Europe's vast primeval forests.

Biologists are pragmatists, students of concrete data and observable phenomena. The British Isles are home to three species of hare, the common hare or brown hare of open farmland (*Lepus europaeus*), the blue or mountain hare of Scotland (*Lepus timidus Scoticus*), and the Irish hare (*Lepus timidus hibernicus*). They have obvious features in common, the lithe body, the powerfully-muscled and elongated hind legs, the prominent eyes set high on the sides of the head, the long and dark-tipped ears. But they vary in size, with the brown hare of southern and lowland Britain by far the largest and heaviest, weighing as much as eight pounds for a mature adult, with ears so long that you can pick up a dead hare and fold its ears forward to extend well beyond the animal's nose, a useful distinguishing test if in doubt about the species. Smaller by a long way is the Irish hare, usually weighing four to six pounds, whose black-tipped ears will barely extend as far as its nose, rabbit-like; and the smallest of the three is Scotland's blue hare, so called because of the bluish tinge of its greyish-dun autumn pelt. Blue becomes white in winter, when Scotland's moorland hares turn snowy-white and acquire a natural camouflage for the high hills in the coldest months. Hares of all species have unusually large hearts and a superabundance of blood, the powerful engine and the high-octane fuel that enables them to leap into such fast, agile and sustained movement.

'I like the hunting of the hare, better than that of the fox', declared Wilfred Scawen Blunt's Old Squire in the poem of the same name: 'New sports I hold in scorn; I like to hunt as my fathers did in the days 'ere I was born.' As a hunter's quarry the hare has held an ancient fascination far surpassing that of foxhunting, an eighteenth century parvenu among field sports, and exceeding in difficulty even the chase of the red deer stag. William Twici, King Arthur's dedicated huntsman, so brilliantly reincarnated in T. H. White's *The Sword in the Stone,* is seized by a kind of mute frenzy when the hunters' talk turns to hare-hunting, his imagination enthralled by the intricate doublings and dodgings of this most mysterious and subtle creature. In early Celtic-British lore and ancient Greek legends alike, the hare is an awesome challenge, a quarry promising difficulties and complexities out of all proportion to its modest size and shy demeanour. The philosopher Xenophon devoted a treatise, the *Cynegeticus*, to hare hunting with scenting hounds in the fourth century B.C. The fifteenth century French and English sporting aristocrats Gaston de Foix and Edward, Duke of York wrote with deferential admiration of the hare as 'the king of all venery . . . the most marvellous beast that is.'

Among early naturalists like Aristotle, Aelian, Pliny and Hippocrates, the hare was a puzzle, a marvellous *lusus naturae*, a quasi-magical animal which seemed to defy all the norms of mammal behaviour. How else could they account for a creature that did not chew the cud, but instead digested its food by re-eating it after excretion? — what biologists call 'refection'. The Jewish dietary taboos set out in Leviticus and Deuteronomy took the hare's habit of refection as a sign of uncleanness, and banned them accordingly. How else but through mystery and magic could ancient commentators explain the phenomenon of superfoetation, whereby a hare can become pregnant again while still bearing the well-developed young from a previous mating, and while suckling the young leverets of her first litter of the year? How else could they interpret the hare's seemingly ambiguous genitalia, which suggested either bisexuality or, to many early naturalists, a bizarre ability to change sex from male to female and back again in successive years?

More than ten centuries later Sir Thomas Browne, a country doctor by profession and a naturalist by inclination in Norwich during the English Civil War, brought an inquiring scepticism and a depth of classical learning to bear upon the mystery of the hare in his tussle with 'vulgar errors' of many kinds, gravely reviewing the ancients' belief that every hare is both male and female '. . . the affirmative of Archelaus, of Plutarch, Philostratus, and many more'. He cautiously concluded that androgyny among hares was at least possible, though not the regular changing of sex from year to year, and recognised the reality of superfoetation, a phenomenon whose workings remained obscure until modern research revealed the physiological means by which hares produce successive overlapping litters of young.

Shakespeare, too, knew about taboos associated with hares, and how their superabundance of blood and their dark flesh signified a preponderance of the melancholy humour. The ebullient Sir John Falstaff, usually so buoyant and jocose, lapses into gloom when talking about 'a hare, or the melancholy of Moor-ditch', while Robert Burton, a contemporary of Browne, cautioned in *The Anatomy of Melancholy* that 'hare is a black meat, melancholy and hard of digestion: it breeds incubus often eaten, and causeth fearful dreams . . . '

Something of the hushed and reverend tones that T. H. White attributes to William Twici when he speaks of hare hunting can still be heard today in the language of some countrymen when hares are discussed. You will find a mixture of respect, apprehension, excitement and a vague unease in their talk. A farm worker who goes beating on a shoot will usually be quick to accept a brace of nice plump rabbits at the end of the day when the bag is divided, but the offer of a hare is likely to produce a polite yet awkward refusal. Many families will not allow the carcase of a hare indoors. In most of Ireland hares are not shot, and even among the rationalist Presbyterians of the Black North there lingers a deeply-rooted unease about hares, perhaps an ancient and unspoken sense that witches may take the shape of hares in daylight.

The hare hunting season in Ireland ends in March, St Patrick's Day on the seventeenth usually marking the day of the last meet, before hounds retire to summer luxury of an idle life and their owners turn to the spring chores of lambing. On the little green fields and the open bogland the hares, which have an extended breeding season from March to September, are regularly to be seen in the bounding, chasing, boxing madness of spring, another aspect of their behaviour that has given rise to widespread lore and legend. What may look like belligerence and rivalry between competing bucks is more often part of the doe's procedure for selecting the male she is to mate with, and the March hares' mad antics are aspects of the animal's behaviour that are now known to take place quite a lot throughout the year. But it peaks in early spring, and is all the more evident to us because of the emptiness of the landscape at this time, with most livestock still kept in, with the first flush of spring grass still to come, and all vegetation at its lowest and most sparse.

Also unknown until quite recently is the extent to which hares will occupy woods and smaller copses, especially by day, an aspect of their secretive lives that was revealed by the modern miracle of telemetry, with scientists tracking wild hares that had been captured and fitted with tiny radio transmitters. Once again, modern scientific methods have proved what many unsystematic field naturalists have previously observed, that cold, wet or stormy weather will bring hares off the open land and into the shelter of the woods. Considering its size, a hare can squat down in a remarkably small depression in the open, such as a ploughed furrow or a natural dip, and can find a surprising degree of shelter from the wind there, just as their cousins the mountain hares will lie-up in the lee of low peaty hags and banks out of the gales. But while these may give shelter from wind and from rain driven on a strong wind, they afford no cover from rain that falls straight and heavily. Exposed thus, a hare's coat will quickly become sodden and turn almost black with its load of moisture, and that is when the woods and their understorey of evergreen shrubs and piles of brashings represent such a valuable shelter, avoiding the chilling that can lead to various respiratory diseases in hares. On the open hills and the vast raised heather bogs long, rank heather performs the same service, and the mountain hares will creep in among the heathery stalks and allow the low canopy of ling to close over them.

Apart from the gregariousness that we often see when spring madness possesses the hares, these animals will sometimes form very large gatherings and live together at astonishing densities. This is especially well documented among Irish hares, and one of their favourite haunts for forming such herds is at airfields and airports. I have a vivid childhood memory of Nutt's Corner, the County Antrim airport that formerly served Northern Ireland, where hundreds of hares lived out on the grassy swards that were intersected by the runways, and where scores of hares raced alongside the old Dakota aircraft as we taxied prior to take-off. The hares would also run along beside aircraft that were taxiing to the terminal after landing, seemingly enjoying all the bustle of airport life, despite the noise of propellers and, later, jets.

And when, in the late 1960s, all commercial air traffic was eventually switched to the new and larger Aldergrove airport a few miles away, the hares migrated en masse to establish themselves there; a direct cross-country migration of an estimated six or seven hundred hares, that immediately settled in and felt quite at home again, surrounded once more by the familiar noises of aircraft comings and goings. What matter if the engines of Rolls-Royce and Pratt & Whitney made the air tremble with the most unpastoral noises, when the place was such a perfect hare habitat in so many other ways, with wide acres of lush grass, free of all sprays and agrochemicals, and a fenced perimeter to exclude foxes and other predators? And just as Pavlov's dogs had learned to salivate when the feeding bell was rung, so the Nutt's Corner hares had learned that the airport din was the noise that meant safety, and then reared innumerable successive generations of hares whose first sensations must have been of aircraft activity.

Like many forms of wildlife on farmland, hares have declined in numbers since the 1960s, especially the formerly abundant brown hares of rich farmland in central and southern Britain, that were so numerous in the 1960s that massive hare shoots were necessary to prevent intolerable damage to growing crops. A medium sized farm might yield a February bag of two hundred hares in one day's shooting, and still produce a similar total the following year. The conditions were ideal for hare abundance, especially in the aftermath of the 1953–54 myxomatosis epidemic, that had wiped out ninety-nine per cent of Britain's rabbits and thereby removed the hare's major competitor for farmland grazing.

By the 1970s hare numbers were falling, a trend that was first observed — perhaps ironically — by followers of hare hunting, beagling and coursing. But you can always rely on practical sportsmen to be sensitive to their prized quarry and its wellbeing. The funds for scientific investigation of the decline came largely as voluntary donations from the hare hunters, and since the 1980s it has become clear that hares have suffered as a consequence of more intensive farming regimes, especially where agrochemical use has been increased, where fields have been enlarged and stripped of hedgerows and small copses, and where vast and boring monoculture acreages of cereals and oilseed rape have replaced the former diversity of mixed arable cropping and livestock grazing, that the hares preferred — and people, too. The hare is unlikely to become rare, or even particularly scarce, in most of Britain in the foreseeable future, but is equally unlikely ever to approach its former abundance unless farmland is managed with greater awareness of the animals' needs. If that can be achieved, the hares will not be the only ones to benefit, because the conditions that promote buoyant hare populations will sustain countless other species of small mammals, birds, plants, wild flowers and insects as well. It is a pleasing prospect, and, given the right approach and the landowners' goodwill, it is a readily achievable one.

A Changeling World

There was an unusual brightness in the first morning light, glimpsed through a narrow gap where the bedroom curtains had not quite been pulled together. Downstairs the kitchen was not exactly cold, but despite the ever-lit Aga it was cooler than usual. I opened the door to let the cascading rush of dogs tumble out for their first romp in the grassy yard, and saw that everything was rimed with frost, steely-pale in the early half-light. The postman arrived, his van's exhaust steaming and smoking in the cold air, his hands gloved against the chill. Over breakfast I went through the daily ritual — junk mail discarded, other items sorted into business and personal, and a quick glance at the newspaper. By now the sun was up, bright and golden, and the trees beyond the kitchen windows stood tall and still in motionless air. The only movement was a swirling but silent clamour of small birds around the feeders of nuts and fatty scraps that dangled from the lower branches of the cherry tree. Occasionally we see a sparrowhawk grab a feeding blue-tit or a siskin here, but we have no right to discriminate: sparrowhawks need to eat, too.

The local squirrels — the native red squirrels, and not the grey tree-rats that show signs of gradually encroaching on the Border country from north and south — have also learned that there is a buckshee meal to be found there when times are hard, and it is not uncommon to see them eagerly devouring peanuts and fatty scraps early in the morning, before the dogs have been let out and they beat an immediate retreat to the safety of the old beeches and the larches beyond. They have a very clear pecking order, too, the largest and oldest squirrels with their darker coloration and prominent ear tufts coming to the food first, and always individually, while the next-in-line waits a little way off, and the others further down the line, including the sandy-tan youngsters, hang about in the old beech hedge and await their eventual turn. They appear to have reached an accommodation with the birds, too, whereby they are allowed to have uncontested dining rights at the wire mesh peanut holder while the tits and siskins concentrate on the breadcrumbs and the scraps of fat. When it is cold and food is scarce, little time and energy is lost in disagreements over who eats what: what matters is just getting on with cramming in the calories.

Booted and jacketed, we set off down the drive and turn right through the hunt gate into the field, the dogs scrambling to get through first, and racing off across the frosted grass down towards the river.

Frost is clean and antiseptic, creating a changeling world. Yesterday that gateway had been thoroughly poached by the passage of horses' hooves, dogs' paws and human footmarks, a bitter-chocolate mousse of ankle-deep mud that now stood stiff and jagged, with frosted patches of white ice in the depressions. Normally we pushed squelchingly through the mud: today we strode firmly over the top of it. Each blade of the rough meadow grass was coated with frosted crystals and looked like a tiny white loofa, or an upright stem of coral. Halfway down the field the lower pond was covered thickly with ice that grumbled as the dogs dashed onto it, slithering and pausing in brief surprise at the cold hard surface where yesterday they had found the more familiar splashy wetness of water, mud and rushes. The ice roared and resonated hollowly as I tapped it with my stick, and where the incoming trickle of the diverted field drain normally dribbled into the pond there was now a long thin icicle that sparkled and winked in the sunlight.

A horse neighed, and we looked back up the hill towards the stables and saw a plume of steam rising vertically from their dunghill, that smoked and smouldered like a doused bonfire in the cold. Horses' heads nodded in recognition over the half-doors of the loose-boxes, their whinnying clear and sharp over two furlongs of white fields. A collie barked from its kennel at a farmhouse almost a mile away beyond the low hill to the south, its high querulous yapping coming clear on the still air.

At the bottom of the field we peered over into the chasm of the river gorge, a gloomy cleft where direct sunlight never penetrates even in midsummer, a damp place of rare ferns and mosses. Far below flowed a ribbon of dark water, a marbled pattern of bottle-greens and steely greys, and the bright gash of white water at the little falls, forbiddingly cold and hostile. On the wooden fence rails there was moss and algae that yesterday would have smeared and coloured our hands and clothes: today it was cold and clean and inoffensive.

Normally the dogs are wet and muddy within minutes of leaving the house, their coats clinging with pond and river water. Today they were dry with their coats fluffed out, all except the young labrador that had rushed impetuously onto the thinner ice of a small pond and crashed through in a spray of ice splinters, romping and revelling despite the icy water.

Along the river's edge are clumps of rushes that usually hold a few snipe. Today, instead of zipping and dodging away with *scaap*-ing zest they sit tight until the dogs are almost on top of them, and then rise with untypical leaden slowness, hardly wavering in flight and pitching down again into another rushy clump about two hundred yards ahead, their behaviour more like that of their skulking, weak-flighted cousins, the jack snipe. After barely three days of cold and twenty-four hours of severe frost the conditions have already begun to weaken them. It seems strange that frost, so invigorating to men and dogs, should make snipe so sluggish, while the usual muggy mildness and murky drizzle of a Scottish winter's day will find them vibrant and active.

Barely five days ago there had been over an inch of rain here in under twelve hours, an unforecast deluge that had swelled the river to a cocoa-coloured, tumbling mass that had risen several feet and lapped at the top of its banks. The subsequent frost, equally unexpected, had clamped its grip on a sodden landscape, halting the seepage from hill drains and burns. The run-off had stopped, the river's current had slackened and lowered, dropping its thick load of suspended sandstone particles, and it now ran with the dark clarity of winter. The banks were fringed with bare trees etched in unnaturally crisp silhouette against the lapis lazuli of the bright sky. The massive trunk of an old beech rises and sprouts into a bouquet of thick boughs, then into slighter branches, then finer twigs and the feathery tufts of tips and shoots. Concentrate, and you can see each line and etched edge. The casual eye usually passes over these details, registering only an impression of a tree's size and shape. 'Jizz' is a good word — originally the military observer's 'general impression of size and shape' — and it nicely sums up the way we normally see the world as a variety of overall impressions, and not the minutiae of components and construction that frosty sunlight makes so clear. If a painter too slavishly picks out the stark lines of these small details that we usually perceive only as an unfocussed haze, it offends the eye. It rebels against the too-gross emphasis of the details we see usually as a blur, shapes at the edges of vision. Painting is not photography, and the living eye does not absorb images like an inert lens and a passive sheet of light-sensitive paper. We live most of our lives by jizz, and not by this altered and unnatural awareness of every line and constituent detail. But this frost and clear air give a temporary extra dimension to vision.

Dogs are a mixed blessing on a country walk. Their dashings and questings a hundred yards and more ahead of us often disturb creatures we might otherwise be able to spot and stalk and study unawares. Their eagerness to race one another down to the river can mean that ducks and kingfishers and dippers will have scattered and made themselves scarce long before we reach the waterside. A dog running ahead along a woodland ride can cause deer and squirrels to move away before we can even glimpse them.

But there are corresponding compensations, thanks to the heightened senses of smell and sight and hearing that dogs enjoy, senses that in man are crude and blunted by comparison. Our little cross-bred terrier, a blend of Lakeland and Border bred in Cumbria by a Lake District foxhunter, works with its black button-nose close to the

ground and is ever ready to detect things that burrow and delve. She alerts us to shrews and field mice in the grass and along the sandy river bank, whose presence we would otherwise miss. The lurcher, a wonderful second-cross miscegenation of whippet, greyhound, deerhound and collie, has not only a keen nose but acute long-sight. She stiffens and stares with the directional intensity of a laser at a shape or movement in the far distance, as a hare scurries up the line of a stone dyke or a fox slips furtively across a field edge. Only a quick hand on her broad collar holds her back from the deep-seated impulse to chase the target she has locked on to. The labradors, with generations of breeding for keen noses behind them, can pick up ground trails and air scents imperceptible to any human nose; while setters and pointers have a virtuoso command of air-borne scents, detecting and signalling the presence of birds and animals sometimes hundreds of yards upwind in a way that is uncanny to see.

'There's nowt so queer as scent, 'cept a woman', remarked Mr John Jorrocks, the Victorian grocer and doyen of all loveable hunting men — and a male chauvinist, as his remark reveals. But in the nineteenth century heyday of his hunting career political correctness had not yet blighted spontaneous freedom of expression; and feminists might even like to consider that Jorrocks was actually acknowledging the inadequacy of the human male in his perplexity when faced with the unfathomable subtleties of womankind. But no-one, male or female, can fathom the mysteries of scent: what is an open book to every dog or fox or deer is forever beyond the ken of a species equipped with such a crude and atrophied sense of smell as man. But we can at least glimpse hints of this other sensory dimension through the way our dogs behave. A huntsman can tell by the feathering sterns of his hounds when they have found a trace of the scent of hare or fox or deer, before that suggestion is confirmed as a certainty when the pack crashes into a full-throated cry. The gundog owner can tell by that quirky cocking of his dog's ears, or the eager circling motion of its tail, when it has sniffed a hint of a rabbit or a hare, quite different from its reaction to a pheasant or a woodcock. And a hunting man can often predict if it's going to be a good scenting day by the behaviour of his dogs when he lets them out for their early run, long before horses are tacked up and horse-boxes loaded for the meet.

Frost often enhances scent for the dogs, though it can also make the ground dangerously hard for them to run on. Lurchers and longdogs can cripple themselves, for their streaking pace and fine-boned build depends upon soft going if toes are not to be dislocated and joints jarred heavily on the iron-hard earth. A setter with its heavily-feathered feet and toes is at an advantage over the comparatively bare-footed pointer, which may feel both the cold and the hardness of the ground too acutely. When the temperature of the earth is a little higher than that of the air scent tends to lie well, which is why foxhunters like to see a touch of frost settling in early on a winter's afternoon. And when scenting conditions are good, the company of a good dog can reveal whole dimensions we would otherwise miss. In woodland, where vision may be limited to just a few yards even in winter, when the leaves are off the trees and the frosts have killed back the undergrowth to its lowest, deer and other creatures are likely to be aware of a human's approach long before we are aware of them, even if we move cautiously upwind, and they slip away unseen. But a dog's nose can be our early warning system; and a steady and experienced dog will turn upwind and stiffen to signal the presence of something ahead, perhaps some way off or maybe just a yard or so beyond our restricted field of view. In either case it is a bonus, putting us on the alert when our attention may have flagged, or if we have been distracted by some other sight or sound.

The use of dogs in woodland is well-established in Germany and France, and also in eastern Europe, and British naturalists and sportsmen are increasingly realising the benefits of having a super-sensitive canine nose as an aid in cover, not simply when shooting or deer culling is going on, but for many kinds of wildlife study, the counting of deer, and the location of ground-nesting birds. No-one who has tried to find the nests of woodcock and pheasants in woodland needs to be reminded how frustratingly difficult it can be, and few who have done it with a good dog will willingly try again without one.

A dog by your side is all very well, but what if it quests out of sight? How, for instance, do you locate your setter when it finds a nest, or a crouching bird, or a deer fawn curled up and motionless, and then sets firmly and silently out of sight? The Europeans have a trick to teach us here, and one which is alien to modern British dogging techniques, although our great-grandfathers would have recognised it. Quite simply, they put a collar and bell on the dog. As the dog works, the bell tinkles; when the dog stops, the bell falls silent. And two dogs can work at the same time, each fitted with a bell of a slightly different tone to the other. The French style of bird-dog bell is called a *grelot*, a truncated triangle of thin brass or copper, the clapper traditionally made from a horseshoe nail. A well-made *grelot* will have a light tone that carries well, and yet its alien metallic sound appears to cause little or no alarm among deer or birds or other wild creatures. It is light in weight, too, and needs only a slender collar from which to hang it; and although a whole generation of British dog handlers have been taught never to run a dog loose in cover with a collar, they can take comfort from the fact that if a dog should chance to become caught by its collar, its tuggings and strugglings will ring the bell and call for assistance. And then, when the dog stops and points its find — a nest or a bird or a deer — you should (as my French friend said, in a magnificent unconscious Irishism) "walk towards the place where the bell is not ringing"!

'As the days get longer, the cold gets stronger.' My father's favourite New Year weather adage is usually reliable, with the hardest frosts of the winter normally reserved for January and February. By the second week of February we began a period of successive freezing nights and chilly days. No snow fell, or even sleet, but the frost was uncompromising, hard and unremitting for eight days and nights. The sodden fields became sheets of ice, concrete-hard underfoot, and unsafe for horsemen. Hunting was cancelled all week, and riders trotted cautiously around the gritted roads in an effort to keep fit horses from fretting in their stables.

On 17 February Judy and I took all five dogs for a walk along the river. An hour later we returned, trudging back up the bottom field, the dogs now a little tired and subdued, trotting only a few yards ahead of us. A narrow field drain, now frozen solid, runs down our western boundary and forms the march of the old kirk glebe, draining from a small ornamental pond at the top of the field. As the dogs moved up the side of the drain, two dark brown birds rose together just ahead of us, not more than ten yards away. They looked like snipe, or perhaps small woodcock, but larger than one and smaller than the other. Their wader characteristics were obvious, with long and sickle-shaped wings and prominent elongated bills. They rose silently and their flight was rather slow and direct, following the uphill line of the drain and the hedgerow towards the pond at the top. Together they dipped out of sight over the crest of the slope. We paused in our tracks, puzzled by what we had seen. Judy has seen hundreds of common snipe and woodcock, and I have seen thousands of both. These birds were like neither.

We called the dogs in to heel and walked on uphill, passing through a wooden slip-gate that leads to the paddock and the upper pond. We were just level with the little earth and rock dam when the two birds rose again from the reedy fringe, much closer this time. Silently and not particularly quickly they rose and swung away from us, gaining height

all the time and turning to fly back down the line of the boundary hedge, but higher and a little further out, over the neighbouring field. They were in sight for perhaps ten or eleven seconds before they rose and breasted the tops of the high beeches and Scots pines that fringe the river gorge, and finally dropped out of sight.

Snipe or woodcock of some sort, definitely: their shapes and coloration left us in no doubt. But these were smaller and more streamlined than woodcock, darker than snipe overall, and with light-coloured tail feathers, and they flew with none of the twisting agility and speed of common snipe, nor with that distinctive *scaape-scaape* on rising. They were like no coastal wader I have ever seen in Europe, nor was the frost severe enough to have driven seashore waders inland from the Solway Firth. The suspicion began to dawn that we had just seen two great snipe. Within minutes we were back indoors, glowing in the sudden heat by the library fire, and thumbing eagerly through field guides and handbooks on snipe and their cousins. The only pictures and drawings of birds that bore a clear resemblance to what we had just seen were, indeed, great snipe. The frost had brought us a clear sighting of two very welcome rarities, the first time I have seen two together, and only my third sighting of great snipe in twenty-five years of winter visits to the marshes where common snipe and jack snipe are common.

On clear frosty winter evenings in January and February sunset comes like a Chinese wash of pastel colours in the west, golds and pinks and oranges. The daylight lasts longer than usual, though we are only a few weeks past the shortest day. We gain almost forty minutes more light than on a more typical grey and overcast evening in a mild February. And after this stolen spell of extra light has ended there still remains a narrow gash of lingering golden-blue on the western edge of the sky when Venus appears, steadfast and untwinkling, already high and bright yellow to the south-west, a warmer and steadier light than the cold and flickering pinpoints of the farther stars.

Protracted periods of unbroken frost can have alarming, even disastrous effects on the more vulnerable birds. When untypically Arctic weather descends and lingers, as in the winters of 1947 and 1963, and to a lesser extent in 1981-82, mortality can be very high. Snipe and herons both depend upon unfrozen wetlands and water margins, and lose weight quickly if they are denied them for more than a few consecutive days. In January 1982 I found a number of herons lying dead by rivers and on frozen marshes, their stiff bodies reduced to a feather-light assemblage of fleshless bones. There was something especially pathetic about these birds, whose sail-winged mastery of flight had dwindled and expired in the unremitting cold. Their long bills, like golden daggers, so deadly at stabbing and spearing at frogs and fish and worms, had been of no avail when faced with thick ice and ground that was as unyielding as concrete. It was fashionable in Victorian and Edwardian times to keep the bills of dead herons and convert them into highly polished cigar and cigarette holders, a fate that would have seemed peculiarly undignified for these wasted victims of the cruel weather.

Wrens can suffer terribly in the prolonged cold, too. We are accustomed to their pert, almost cocky shapes in the winter hedgerows and among the marshland rushes, but their little bodies are too inefficient at conserving energy to withstand extended periods of sub-zero temperatures. Wren numbers were recorded as having crashed dramatically after the winters of 1947 and 1963, and in early 1982 I saw several instances of how the hard-pressed birds would congregate at unusually large communal roosts, huddling together to conserve as much heat as they could. One such, and an unlikely find, was in the derelict remains of an old brick privy in the overgrown garden of a derelict cottage in Ireland. The door of rotting timber and flaking paint hung limply askew from the remains of one hinge, and a rich tangle of ivy had invaded the interior, smothering the walls and wrapped around the rusty pipes and the old cistern. Huddling there, almost like a swarm of tawny bees, were scores of wrens, perhaps a hundred or more, packed together into the dark nooks and corners away from the cold white world outside.

The Fringe of the Moor

Heads seem scarcely to have touched pillows when a firm tapping on the bedroom door had us lurching back into bleary-eyed and tentative wakefulness. The gap in the curtains revealed just the faintest hint of first light, and the effects of hot tea gradually affirmed a surer grasp of the realities of early dawn. Warm clothes, a road map, cameras, binoculars and a stalker's telescope were gathered; and then the car headlights lit up the yard of our friends' farm on Deeside. Rabbits' eyes glinted from the gloom on either side of the farm track, and bobbing white scuts jinked out of our way. At the road junction a roebuck in the field opposite was caught fleetingly in the headlights' glare, standing hock deep in the early grass, head erect and watchful as we swept by, his newly-clean antlers showing ivory white, his coat still the greyish-dun of late winter.

On the miles of single-track road there was a sparse scattering of rabbit corpses, victims of the few cars that had passed that way the night before, with carrion crows already in attendance, ready to breakfast on these easy pickings. On the heathery slope to our right above the road a short-eared owl was quartering the hill with silent dedication, and a cock hen-harrier rose like a silver-grey wraith from a roadside swathe of young bracken, to swing away with loose-winged insouciance on the chill breeze.

Eight miles of driving brought us to within a hundred yards of the hill stream, where the road swung right and followed the little glen westwards, with a sprinkling of rowans between the road and the river, and a mantle of birches and young larches girdling the lower slopes of the heather to our right. The little river — more than a mere burn by now — veered off to our left, running close below a slope of heathery grasses interspersed with birch and small Scots pines, and leaving a wide arcing swathe of short grass and dwarf willow between the road and the bubbling water. The car slowed by some low gorse clumps and swung gently off the road, coming to rest facing the river and the rising ground beyond.

Already the black grouse were there. No more than a hundred yards away, on the grassy lawn by the sweeping bend of the river, there was a scattering of black dots, easily visible now in the clear light. Car windows were wound down gently, binoculars trained and focussed on the green amphitheatre in front of us. Across an area of perhaps two acres of grass we counted sixteen black grouse cocks, grouped loosely in twos and threes. They seemed passive and almost inert, apart from an occasional scuttling run and the quick flickering of wings that were extended and folded again. Then the fitful breeze swung in our favour, blowing from the birds towards us, and bringing a gentle bubbling *continuo* of soft sounds not unlike the muted coo-ing of doves, but sustained at an unmodulated level as if a machine were throbbing: the velvet-smooth humming and coo-ing of displaying blackcock.

Every minute or two we made another count of the birds, and gradually their numbers grew as one black shape after another glided in, following the river's course on set wings, and pitching among the others on their grassy parade ground. As the gathering increased in size the bubbling and coo-ing, and the physical activity, steadily became more animated. The sound was steady and unhesitating, seeming never to pause for breath, and burbling gently like some piece of powerful and smooth-running machinery. The grouse began to assume better defined small groups, with two or three birds confronting one another a few yards apart from the next little gathering; and in less than half an hour there were twenty-nine blackcock in all, divided into eleven little sub-committees. The black of their plumage — actually more of a deep steely-blue now in the better light and the binoculars' images — showed up starkly against the grasses; but most vivid of all were the continual flashes of white from the birds' wing-bars and the rounded feather-duster tufts of their under-tail covert feathers. Erect, fluffed out, and gleaming with an almost silvery purity, they made a conspicuous and unmistakeable contrast against the blue-black of the cocks' bodies and the arcing sable blades of their curved and fanned-out tail feathers. A pair of 7x-magnification binoculars easily picked up the rowan-berry-red wattles over each bird's eyes, while the 24x- stalking telescope made these appear like the segment shapes of tangerines but coloured a full-blooded red, and arching dramatically over each eye, like outsize crimson blinkers that had slipped up awkwardly and assumed the position of brightly rouged eyebrows, with the blackish-brown of the bird's crown forming a dark furrow between them.

The birds' postures were uncompromising and confrontational, each squaring up directly to his nearest neighbour, head lowered and thrust forward, with a fluffed-out mantle of dark neck and throat feathers, backs horizontal, and tails and wings outstretched, flared and drooping. Their physical attitudes were a mixture of decisive, energetic aggression and self-conscious 'Look at me!' exhibitionism. Mankind's seeming artifices often mirror nature, and here at the black-grouse lek the extravagant males in their breeding finery were putting on a vigorous display of posturing and stylised aggression for the benefit of the females with which they would shortly mate, while the sombre and well-camouflaged hen birds waited and watched discreetly at a distance, shortly to mate with the dominant cocks and slip away to begin the solitary female business of nesting, egg laying, incubation, and the rearing of the young. It is fashionable and 'politically correct' for western societies to forswear gender stereotypes, to scorn the vying of males for sexual dominance over females, to hail an equality and interchangeability of roles and genders; but these grouse of the woodland edges and the moorland fringes behave in a way that anthropologists can find in many human cultures, as the males dance and display overtly in a continual state of stand-off enmity, while the quietly passive females wait and watch on the periphery of the arena as a prelude to pairing, then to be followed by the wearisome and unspectacular chores of motherhood and the production of a new generation that, in their turn, will do just the same.

There were a few dull brown shapes of greyhens scattered motionless here and there among the tufted deer grass and stunted willow, and two were perched in the branches of a birch tree that overlooked the lek, and there were probably many more so well concealed or camouflaged that we missed them.

By 7.30 a.m. the gathering, and the emollient coo-ing, seemed to be at its height, when the birds suddenly rose, first one or two, then a steady trickle of others, and flew with slow and powerful wingbeats across the river, sweeping along the steeply-sloping heathery hillside for a couple of hundred yards, and then dropping suddenly into the long heather. Four or five took stand in the branches of a blasted Scots pine, while another handful alighted on a small patch of grassy 'white ground', their dark shapes obvious to us even at over four hundred yards distance. Was that it? Was the matinée performance over for today, perhaps only to recur in a smaller, briefer form towards dusk? The grassy arena was deserted now, and all my telescope revealed was a scattering of feather fragments where clashing wings had been damaged, or where bits of primaries had been broken off as the birds dragged their stiffly drooping wings along the ground in their daily displays.

Then, as suddenly as they had gone, and for no reason that we could detect, some of the cocks began to drift back to the lek, first one or two, then a steady trickle, until we could once again count fifteen birds on the grass. The others had gone for today, it seemed, and never re-appeared to join these. They stood about almost nonchalantly, much less agitated and animated than before, and seemingly content just to eye one another, with only an occasional hint of that coo-ing refrain. We watched for another twenty minutes, and then the last of the lekking party finally began to disperse, rising individually and each disappearing on its own with a heavy purposeful flight up or down the stream and out of sight.

Now, in the first week of May, the same dawn and dusk displays would be taking place daily at scores of lek sites across Scotland and the north of England, almost always on just such a level swathe of grass, usually on the fringes where moorland meets the woods, or in level clearings among the more geometrical regimentation of the conifer forests. For birds that are so well camouflaged and usually secrete themselves so effectively among low vegetation, the lek is a surprising piece of exhibitionism. The most detailed lek studies have been made in Scandinavia and northern Europe, where this generally declining species still occurs in good numbers, but the various social and breeding functions of the lek are not yet fully understood. But it clearly gives an opportunity for rival cock birds to meet and, through confrontation, to determine their relative dominant and sub-dominant positions in the local population, and to attract the attention of sexually receptive females with which they will mate within a short distance of the lekking ground. A dominant blackcock will mate successively with a number of hens, and these then slip quietly back to their individual pre-selected nesting areas, where, having performed his role, the male takes no further part in the hatching and rearing of the young. Still unknown is the extent to which these repeated and sometimes frenzied cocks' displays are also necessary to induce sexual receptiveness among the greyhens.

Lekking sites are, in many instances, very old and have been seen to be used annually for many decades. This continuity is believed to be important for the social structure and breeding success of black grouse, so it is all the more alarming when a change in land use, such as forestry or road building, causes a lek site to be ploughed up or tarmaced over. Black grouse were formerly present right across Britain, from Cornwall to Caithness, but their range has shrunk and their numbers dwindled steadily since mid-Victorian times. Bag records are known to be a reliable index of game abundance, and the record British black grouse bags came from Cannock Chase in Staffordshire and from Dumfriesshire, both in the 1860s. Today they are extinct in Staffordshire and scarce in Dumfriesshire, for reasons we cannot entirely identify. More intensive agriculture and forestry regimes are undoubtedly the main causes of decline, and as a species the black grouse may be unusually susceptible to even quite minor habitat changes. Rivalled only by the plight of the grey partridge, black grouse declines across all its former range in Europe and western Asia have been a growing cause for concern among game biologists.

The moorland fringes that black grouse love are also one of the best habitats in which to have a chance of glimpsing a much less conspicuous creature, the wildcat. In countless paintings, especially Victorian studies of the Landseer type, and in many photographs, usually of captive individuals, the wildcat is portrayed as a furious feline demon, glaring, hissing, and spitting with low-set ears flattened back, and with teeth and mouth exposed in a cruel rictus of venom. Successive generations of taxidermists have copied these models, and you can safely bet that every stuffed wildcat whose glazed eyes blaze out from glass cases in Highland hotels or lodges has much the same expression, like a diminutive Caledonian tiger cornered and poised to spring.

In the wild the reality is rather different, where wildcats, like every wild feline, will slip away quickly at any hint of an approaching human, always preferring evasion to confrontation. If you are lucky, you may sit quietly by a plantation at dawn or dusk and see a wildcat going about its methodical hunting, moving with a stealth and sinuous elegance that is rather similar to that of a fox, until it is swallowed up again in the long heather, grasses and trees, or a swirling wind puffs a hint of your scent in its direction and sends it racing for cover. Two of my best sightings of wildcats were out on the open heather in broad daylight, once when I was trekking towards a distant hill loch and my labrador flushed a magnificent wild tomcat from his resting place among some dwarf willows, and once when we were dogging for grouse, when a steady old pointer quivered to a statuesque halt and pointed something just upwind, her ears cocked and her tail describing a curious rotating movement that betokened something quite different from the intended covey of grouse. Only when she was sent in to flush did we see a scuttling dark shape with a short and bushy tail ringed with broad dark bands, that raced away ahead of the puzzled dog, streaking *ventre à terre* across a broad expanse of open heather until it vanished into a clump of distant birches.

Until someone undertakes some much-needed research it will be impossible to tell whether the wildcats of northern Scotland are rare and in decline, as some people will contend, or numerous and increasing, as others will argue with equal conviction. My own impression, based on nothing more systematic than a handful of sightings, a variety of signs and tracks, and conversations with keepers, landowners, stalkers and foresters, is that they are probably increasing, especially in areas where there has been recent

afforestation. The dark and silent blocks of softwoods, together with the cessation of traditional gamekeepering that usually accompanies it, seem to create suitable conditions for a secretive carnivore that will benefit where it has seclusion and cover close to open moorland and the birds and animals that live there.

In according formal protection to *felis sylvestris scoticus*, the true indigenous wildcat of the Highlands, there are major problems of identification to overcome, stemming largely from their ability and readiness to interbreed with domestic cats, or their feral progeny. In the Highlands domestic moggies are legion, and a proportion of these will go native and take to living off the land. I have several times encountered superb wild cats — as distinct from wildcats — right out in the hills and many miles from any house or road, including one magnificent brindled tomcat that we encountered in a remote corner of Skye, in the very act of taking young grouse chicks. He and his like will readily mate with true wildcats, and with the resultant hybrid progeny, and the consequence is frequent confusion about whether or not an individual specimen is a true wildcat or not. The immediate diagnostic signs to look for are a short, thick tail hooped with broad dark rings, and a flattened skull with low-set ears, but those alone are not always enough, and many a cat taken in a keeper's trap or found dead as a road casualty cannot be identified with complete certainty. Perhaps the magic of genetic fingerprinting is really the only way to find the correct answer.

As for the traditional perceptions of cornered or captive wildcats being devils incarnate, I will not argue on that score. On two occasions I have had the dubious privilege of handling wildcat kittens that had to be inoculated by a vet — one lot were almost certainly true wildcats, and the others were clearly wild-feral crossbreds — and I have never seen so much unbridled fury and energy and blind manic frenzy packed into such little bundles of fur. They hissed and spat like demons, and two pairs of heavy gauntlets worn over a thick padded jacket seemed barely sufficient to resist their biting, clawing, writhing aggression. Old hands have told me that wildcats make excellent pets if you can find and start to tame a litter of kittens before their eyes are open; but I am curiously reluctant to put their recommendations to the test.

The Hunters of the Cliffs

The basalt plateau rises abruptly from the sea, leaving only a narrow littoral of a few hundred yards between the waves and the dark rampart of the cliffs. There is a deep cleft in the cliff face, a deep V of cloven rock where a steady rivulet of bubbling water spills down, the steady seepage from the blanket peat on the flat top of the plateau. After a few hours of sustained heavy rain it will swell to a tumbling deluge, always speedily responsive to the rainfall, yet never drying up even in the longest summer droughts, thanks to the steady drainage from the blanket bog that trickles down over black rocks cloaked in emerald green mosses.

At the foot of the cleft there is just enough room to park a small car off the road, and there is a steep and narrow path leading upwards to the right of the cleft. To call it a path is to exaggerate its definition and the extent to which it is used. It is more of a natural route that is negotiable by carefully placed human feet, and seldom traversed by anyone other than the occasional hill walker or bird-watcher. Few people know it exists; the coastal road whisks cars past too quickly, and even the little pull-in might seem too small to park a car. Gritty and sometimes loose underfoot, the way up is mostly firm and safe, if you have a reasonable head for heights and a good sense of balance. It is a stiff climb to the top, almost a hands-and-knees scramble at times, when you are grateful for the occasional firm-rooted tussock of heather as a temporary handhold. Near the top, about six hundred feet above the road and the sea, the gradient eases and the way widens. The tight cleft of the gully opens out as a gently sloping sweep of heather and tumbled rocks, an area a little larger than a billiard table, and sheltered from above by an overhanging hag of peat fringed with heather, woodrush and rough grasses. Here you stop, straighten up, rest protesting leg muscles and pumping lungs, and turn around to look back and down to where the sea foams below, and away towards the distant silhouette of Ailsa Craig, like a great haystack chiselled out of grey granite, and the further outline of the Irish coast twenty miles or so to the west across the North Channel.

Ahead of you, stretching far inland, lie miles of heathery moorland and high grassy sheepwalks, dotted at wide intervals with a scattering of blackfaced sheep, and home to a moderate population of grouse, though you will need to be fit to walk them up, or have a team of wide-quartering setters or pointers to quest and locate them. In spring the plateau is a busy place, alive with nesting birds. Curlews float and bubble on the wind, and there are lapwings and occasional oystercatchers too, and the level ground is busy with the activities of skylarks and wheatears and meadow pipits, all the spring returnees that revitalise the moors after the silence and emptiness of late winter as they come north again from Africa, Spain and France from late March onwards.

And with them return the merlins. These little falcons usually forsake the high moors in autumn, some travelling as far south as France, Spain and Portugal for their winter quarters, others merely moving down onto low farmland and estuaries where there is a good supply of prey all winter in the form of small passerines and waders. And each spring they return to nest here, and the heathery space at the top of the cleft is their favourite site. Here they have shelter from the wind that sweeps incessantly over the open moors, a south-west exposure that can make this a sun-trap on a bright day, and the long view that is so often found where merlins choose their ground nesting sites.

Elsewhere, especially to the east in Galloway, which has more afforested land than any other part of Britain, the merlins are tree nesters, fond of the abandoned structures of crows and magpies. But here on the open moorland plateau they nest in a depression in the ground, among heather and a scattering of small boulders.

The little merlin has an elegance, a finesse and an agility on the wing that are unsurpassed by any other resident British raptor, and only the little hobby, a summer visitor from the south, can rival its delicate energy. Merlins combine the stealth and low-level speed of a sparrowhawk with the high-mounting, fast, stooping dash of the peregrine. They will execute a lightning smash-and-grab attack with all the low-level energy and surprise of a sparrowhawk, swinging round a knoll or bursting over a low skyline like a tiny fighter aircraft, avoiding the ground defences of a pipit or a wheatear until it is too late for the prey to move and save itself. For the skylark, its favourite spring and summer prey, it will mount in a high, ringing flight, like some relentless projectile that has locked itself onto its quarry. This contention between merlin and skylark has an ancient and natural inevitability, and has always been one of the most spectacular sights for the watcher of wild falcons, and also for the skilled falconer who has been able to train his captive merlin to the peak of fitness and determination, to pursue its wild and elusive prey in a ringing flight that may take them so high that even binoculars cannot pick them up. The old tradition was for merlins to be taken as eyasses from the nest, to be entered on prey like pipits, and finally to be released into the wild in early autumn after proving their self-reliance in these testing flights at skylarks. Today the skylark and the merlin both enjoy the law's protection, and a special licence is required for a registered falconer to fly his merlins — almost certainly captive-bred — at skylarks, a curious intervention of bureaucracy in an age-old encounter between hawk and prey.

Some of the finest displays of the little merlins' agility and aggression can be seen when a pair defend their nesting site against the incursions of what they perceive as a rival. I remember a grey day in early April, when I stopped the car and used my binoculars to sweep the heathery hillside for any sign of the merlins that I knew had nested there for several seasons past. There was no sign of them. Then, overhead, there was the deep and guttural croak of a carrion crow, a single bird that flapped steadily on its straight flightpath northwards across the deep glen. It flapped onwards on its purposeful yet seemingly weary way, and its occasional bass croaking was suddenly joined by a high, shrill, rapidly repeated *kekk*-ing, a cry of fury and outrage from a merlin that swung into flight from the steep heather and flickered upwards on narrow, pointed wings. It was almost immediately joined by another, shrieking the same wheezy-shrill note of rage. All three birds were now clear in the narrow scope of the binoculars' image, the crow now looking even more cumbersome and leaden in flight compared with the agile manoeuvrings of this pair of assailants. They wheeled and swooped and circled the flapping black shape, darting after it with the co-ordinated deadliness of purpose of two greyhounds after a hare, each taking its turn to climb and stoop fast at the crow, then pulling up and avoiding contact barely an inch above its black back. The lightness and speed of their blurred and shallow wingbeats and their aerobatic ease was emphasised by the steady flap-flap of the lumbering crow, that scarcely reacted to their frenzied onslaught and was not to be deflected from its relentless northward course. It seemed to take their onslaught with a tired and passive resignation, like a ponderous heavyweight boxer weathering a succession of lightning blows from two nimble flyweights.

Merlins' aggression and the noisy aerial ways they express it often give away the birds' presence early in the spring, which is a bonus for the hawkwatcher in his quest for nesting pairs. Later, during incubation, this self-advertising activity is often replaced by an equal dedication to furtiveness and stealth, the female often content to sit tight on her eggs, motionless in her camouflaged silence, even when a seemingly threatening intruder comes within feet of her. I know of one pair that have bred successfully for several successive seasons at a nest site in long heather and mossy scree less than five yards from a well-worn hill track, traversed by thousands of pairs of heavy-booted feet each spring from Easter onwards, the female sitting as inert and indistinguishable as one of the mossy granite rocks that surround her as the endless parties of noisy, brightly-dressed ramblers trek past.

In winter we often see merlins among the low, flat fields that fringe the Solway Firth. Probably these are the same birds that nest in spring in the vast afforested uplands of Galloway, within sight to the north and west, where so much study has been devoted to their ways and the continuing mystery of their slow decline, when all other British raptor populations are stable or on the increase. They perch and rest and preen on the tops of the square wooden fence posts; or we glimpse them in headlong flight after a meadow pipit or among a wheeling, screaming cloud of small waders along the mudflats. They have their communal roosts on this coastal plain, too, where four or five merlins may spend the long dark hours among a group of low birches or willows; and we sometimes find their plucking posts, perhaps an old railway sleeper now doing duty as a stout corner straining post for a wire fence, or a raised rocky knoll overlooking the level fields, where a scattering of small feathers and a limp collection of bones indicates where a dunlin, a plover or a snipe has been stripped of all its flesh by the merlin's toothed bill, wielded hungrily yet with the minute delicacy of a surgeon's scalpel.

Two other haunters of these cliffs and the flat moorlands above them are the buzzards and the ravens. I usually think of them together, since I so often see both in the sky together, the raven flying a steady and purposeful course towards some distant destination, or perhaps tumbling and circling with one or two others, while the buzzards soar and glide in wide spirals on the gentle thermals of warm spring days, or hover in the updraught from the cliffs, wide and mothlike wings set motionless and giving only the occasional lazy flap.

These are year-round residents, well able to withstand the rigours of a moorland winter when there is so much ready feeding in the form of sheep carrion and the occasional deer carcase, and rabbits among the rocky screes for the buzzards. Walter, the retired shepherd, can remember the days early this century when a small army of gamekeepers patrolled these moors and crags, paid to preserve the grouse at all costs. Ravens and buzzards were automatically seen as villainous competitors, although they actually did no significant harm, and the landowners and their agents expected to see their remains hanging from the vermin gibbets that each keeper had to maintain on his beat, as grim evidence that he was doing his job. Few thought to question their orders, or dared to, mindful of the long dole queues of the depression that followed the first world war.

However important grouse management was, these moors were never wholly given over to sport. Integrated land use was practised, in the form of low to medium density sheep farming, which is still a good combination where traditional heather management and careful shepherding are carried on. Like the shooters and the keepers, the shepherds saw the ravens and the buzzards as a threat, since both are fond of feeding on sheep and lamb carrion. As a shepherd walked his beat with his dogs, the sight of a raven or a buzzard rising from a dead sheep was enough in itself to brand the birds as sheep killers in his eyes, even though neither could possibly overpower and kill a healthy sheep, preferring to dine on a stillborn or sickly lamb or a dead carcase, or, in the raven's case, to attack a weak or dying animal that had couped and was unable to rise again. And so the shepherds supported the keepers' war against both these birds. Walter tells me that a favourite ploy of the keepers, especially in the hungry months of late winter and early

spring, was to lace a sheep's carcase with strychnine procured from the local molecatcher, and suspend it over the cliff on a rope. Here the lethally-dosed carrion was safely out of the way of dogs and humans, but still readily accessible to the scavenging ravens and buzzards, whose corpses would later be collected, ramrod-stiff in the spasms of strychnine poisoning and the rigor of death, from the foot of the sheer rock wall. The occasional hill fox and stoat would fall victim, too, having scrambled down the rocks to reach the enticing, rotting flesh, and so be added to the unending vermin tally.

It was a war of attrition that neither side ever won or lost: intensive keepering and predator control may have maintained high grouse stocks for the Guns, but the predators were never eliminated. Instead their population was kept in check but remained healthy, like a coiled spring that was ready to bounce back to a more natural level when the pressure eased, as happened when war broke out and the keepers were conscripted. It took the invisible and insidious effects of pesticides from the 1950s onwards to do real and potentially permanent damage to many predatory species. And the buzzards' regular and favourite prey, the rabbit, was hit for six by the arrival of the myxomatosis virus in 1953, which swept like an angel of death through British rabbit populations and killed ninety-nine per cent of them in a couple of years. Adaptation was the key to survival, and the depleted numbers of buzzards learned to concentrate on sheep carrion, and to turn to new alternatives like field voles, earthworms and frogs, in the absence of the once-abundant rabbit. By 1990 the rabbit numbers were back to something near pre-myxomatosis levels, and were once again the most prominent item in the buzzards' diet.

Here, where trees are few and crags abound, the ravens and buzzards are both cliff nesters, and eager competitors for the best nest sites. Both are early nesters, among the very earliest of all British birds, and they can be seen — and heard — actively contesting ownership of cliff nesting places from February onwards. Their aerial combats are especially conspicuous, for these are both big birds with distinctive, far-carrying calls. In February, however bad the weather, and even as early as January in a mild winter, ravens and buzzards will vie for nesting sites for long hours, repeatedly swooping and calling and tumbling and diving at each other; the buzzard uttering its high, enraged, yet always plaintive calls, while the raven goes through its wide repertoire of *basso profundo* croaks, high yaps and gravelly barks and *cronk*-ing grunts. Somehow, casualties or even direct physical clashes are rather rare, and noise and energetic bluster is the chief tactic on both sides.

Eventually, an accommodation is reached, and by mid-March most female ravens will have laid their eggs and be sitting tight, often despite gales and snow and heavy rain, to hatch their helpless young in the first half of April. Then the male's job is to roam the moors for the remains of sheep carrion, and later with flesh from young lambs that have succumbed on the hill, packing his crop for regurgitation back at the nest to feed his mate and the young. A raven's nest may begin with a clutch of five or six eggs, but the number of young that survive to fledge successfully depends heavily upon the availability of food. Two or three fledgelings in a normal year, perhaps, with four well-reared young in seasons when food has been plentiful and the weather conditions good. The size of the fledged brood is almost always a reflection of the abundance or scarcity of food, with the young hatched out into the hostile and bleak weather of the uplands at just the time when carrion is usually at its most abundant.

The buzzards, like the ravens, build sturdy but rather unkempt nests on their chosen ledges, wedging sticks into crannies in the rocks, and then adding a finer lining of smaller twigs, sheep's wool, feathers, tufts of heather and strands of woodrush, the completed nest continually refreshed with new greenery from time to time as the eggs are being incubated, and often after the young have hatched. Nest building can be a prolonged affair for buzzards, taking place gradually over a period of as much as six or seven weeks before the first eggs appear, and it seems to be a part of the general manoeuvrings and displays whereby a chosen site is marked out and defended in preparation for the eventual laying of the eggs — usually three and occasionally four — and the start of the five-week incubation period. Food availability is critical for the survival of the young buzzards, too, and when it is scarce the survival chances are best for the strongest individual, usually the first to hatch. In a year of plenty all the chicks may fare well, and in two successive years I returned in early July to see both adults soaring in the cliffs' updraught, accompanied by four juveniles.

One evening in late September I had a telephone call from Walter. One of the local shepherds had been out on the hill and come across a buzzard that appeared to have a broken wing. He had wrapped the hissing, clawing, protesting and terrified bird in his tweed jacket and carried it down off the heather to his car, and delivered it to Walter, who has a local reputation as 'the birdman'. He knew I had been a falconer, so could I help?

On my hour-long car journey I stopped twice and quickly picked up two road-casualty carcases, a rabbit and a well-grown leveret, thinking of the disabled buzzard's likely need for food. She — it turned out to be a young female — was ensconced, quietly and with something almost approaching contentment, in a converted chicken coop, the wire netting covered with thin laths of wood to prevent her from dashing her head and bill

against it. She had therefore remained unmarked by the usual stigmata of a captive wild raptor, a bleeding head and damaged cere above the base of the bill. I cut a meaty leg off the hare and slipped it, partially skinned, into the cage, as the bird flattened itself in the far corner away from me, her eyes blazing in defiance mixed with pain and bewilderment. An hour later I looked in on her before I left for home, and she was pulling with gusto at the meat, grasping it in her feet and ripping upwards with power and evident appetite.

The story unfolded by Walter's fireside. The young shepherd had found the bird, flapping in a patch of old heather and unable to rise, just a couple of hundred yards away from the line of high cables and skeletal pylons that march in an ugly line across the moors. The broken wing, fractured at the knuckle, was a typical result of a collision with wires, an accident that many young birds encounter, and raptors probably more than most. By noon next day a vet with a special enthusiasm for falconry and birds of prey had called and collected her, and she was on her way for an X-ray, treatment and life in a recuperation aviary. Though still in immature plumage, by the time of her September accident she was fully grown and already an accomplished hunter, able to fend for herself, so there was a good chance that she could be returned to life in the wild. By late February she had been released, at a spot barely two miles from where Walter's friend had found her, fully fit once again, but now marked with an unobtrusive BTO identification ring of light alloy on one leg and an eyecatching plain circlet of bright blue on the other, so we could identify her at a distance. All that year the local birders and keepers saw her regularly along the line of coastal cliffs and inland over the hills, and in the following spring she paired and nested on a crag just eight miles north of the scene of her accident, rearing two young.

Creatures of a Day

As April gives way to May, with longer days and rising air and water temperatures, new natural events occur on many British rivers, Irish loughs and a surprising number of Scottish lochs too, especially where these are not too acidic or devoid of shoreline vegetation and shelter. The mayflies begin to emerge, to the delight of the black-headed gulls and various insect-eating birds, of the trout — and of trout flyfishers. Up to two years have been spent in the larval stages of life, out of sight in the water's depths, beginning as a fertilised egg which is laid upon the water's surface by the dipping female. This sinks to its eventual resting and growing place among the river gravels or amid the marls and mud and rocks of the lough bed, to develop into a nymph, the larval stage of the insect's life, which burrows and crawls in silt and fine gravels, and lives in burrows of its own making, and feeds among the rich debris of decayed vegetable matter that litters the bed of the lake, and on the algae that coats the stones and pebbles. Mayfly nymphs are the only insect larvae that burrow, and they have the distinctive three tails that are so conspicuous in their later dun and spinner stages.

Within about two weeks the tiny mayfly egg has begun to grow into a nymph and feed on the lake or river bottom. As it grows it repeatedly sheds its outer skeleton, and two years of secretive, largely unseen growth are crowned by its eventual appearance at the surface, when it has swum upwards towards the surface and the light. There it struggles eagerly in the surface film in the desperate throes of eclosion, the skin of the larva bursts and slips away as the new life within wrenches itself free, to reveal itself in the delicate elegance of the emergent mayfly dun. There is no mistaking this dun form, which is by far the largest upwinged fly found in the British Isles, with a wingspan of more than five centimetres, and three slender and elongated tails which are slightly upswept. Hatching mayfly are best seen out on the still waters of a lake, where there is no current to whisk the mayfly downstream and out of sight, and a boat makes a comfortable floating observation platform.

On the surface appears the larva, which twitches and spins in the clinging meniscus as the insect inside fights to release itself from the confines of the larval case. The mayfly is at its largest, most helpless and most vulnerable to a predator in the form of a feeding trout or a swooping insect-eating bird just as the last stage of emergence is in progress, when its body size is emphasised by the extension of the still-clinging case or shuck, and therefore its visibility to predators is at its maximum. The larval case adds greatly to the insect's length and clings to the water's surface film, holding the mayfly down on the surface until it finally fights its way fully free, and opens its wings for the first time, to dry and reveal their lacy, prominently-veined veils of greyish-green. On some rivers and lakes these are decidedly yellowish in colour, even a light primrose, while on others they are much duller, a subtle pale pastel lovat-green or a lichen-like greyish-green. Can these be distinct local variants, races, or even subspecies? Yet we are told by all the reference books that there are only three mayfly species in the British Isles, one of which, the *lineata*, is so scarce that it hardly counts. *Danica* is the familiar mayfly of Irish loughs and Scottish lochs, of tarns and lakes in northern England, and of the chalk streams that stretch from Yorkshire and Derbyshire to Hampshire, Wessex and Kent. *Vulgata* is less common, though still not rare, and tends to take the place of *danica* on small lakes and ponds with muddy bottoms, and on more sluggish waters, and is not so avidly sought as prey by trout and birds.

The mayfly is also the only insect that emerges in one form, the dun, and then undergoes a further moult before it mates and dies as a spinner. The dun form has visible but non-working mouthparts, which proclaim that its feeding days are over and the end of its life is near. The male dun's reproductive organs are also covered and useless at this stage, but both sexes' wings are fully functional, and the hatched mayfly only remains on the surface of the water for as long as it takes for its wings to dry and allow it to rise and fly off. Drying and eventual lift-off come quicker on a breezy day than when the atmosphere is humid and still, and the trout may feed on emergent mayflies in differing ways according to the conditions. When there is a large hatch in progress, and a dry and breezy atmosphere allows the insects to dry out and flutter off quickly, the trout will often tend to feed little if at all on the surface, on fully-emerged insects, and may concentrate instead on voracious feeding below the surface on the upward-swimming nymphs. Bulging sub-surface movements may be all you can see of fish activity at times like this. But when there is a steady hatch of mayflies on a humid day the trout have plenty of time to see the emergent insects struggling on the surface and waiting for their wings to dry in the still, damp air, and they pick off their flies with a powerful swirling rise, grabbing the mayflies as they surge up through the surface, and then turning down and away to swallow them.

Poor mayfly! Her first Latin name is *Ephemera*, 'the creature with just one final day of life', 'the transient or fleeting one', and she is indeed an insect of no more than a couple of days of life at most, in this final and most visually attractive stage of her development. (There are males and females, of course, but we always seem to refer to the mayfly as 'she', as an appreciation of its grace and delicacy.) This combination of the ephemerid insects' delicate beauty and fleetingly brief life has become a byeword, a metaphor for the transitoriness of all beauty, and a beauty that is all the more poignant and precious because of its impermanence.

After hatching, and as soon as it can use its wings, the mayfly rises with a flickering motion and makes its way to the nearest bankside or shoreline vegetation as directly as the wind will allow it. There it rests on the leaves of trees and bushes, usually clinging to the underside of the vegetation, which gives it some shelter from wind and rain, reduces dehydration, and conceals it from the gaze of predators. It has always been traditional for trout fishers to try and tempt their fish by using the natural insect as bait, as well as the many artificial imitations that are made from feathers and fur and hair. Dapping — the technique of bobbing a fly on the surface of the water, as the wind carries out the line from the tip of the angler's rod — is a very ancient method that the Macedonians of pre-Christian times knew, and that was used for centuries in Britain and Europe when crude and stiff fishing rods could do little more than dangle a line over the water, relying on the wind to lift and carry the line and the fly, before the development of rods and lines that could cast and propel a fly. Dapping the natural mayfly is still important and effective as a flyfishing technique, especially on the large limestone loughs of central and western Ireland; and the local schoolchildren supplement their pocket money each morning in late May and early June by collecting scores of mayflies from the undersides of the leaves of the shoreline thorn bushes and alders, and selling them to visiting flyfishers eager for dapping baits.

Like all insects that hatch from a watery environment, mayflies are sensitive to temperature and their behaviour is largely dictated by the temperature of the water and the air. A period of cold weather can delay the onset of the annual hatch, by days and sometimes by weeks. Fishing pilgrims to the Irish mayfly loughs trust in the general reliability of traditional dates, and on the earliest waters like Lough Derg and Lough Arrow they will expect to see good hatches of mayflies and evidence of active trout feeding by 17 May. But on these big loughs every bay has its own microclimate, and the warmer and more sheltered areas will usually experience the first hatches of mayflies several days earlier than other colder and more exposed parts of the loughs, even in a typical spring. Exceptionally warm weather early in spring has sometimes caused mayfly hatches to begin as early as the end of April on some waters, as happened throughout the British Isles in 1938, while cold and stormy May weather can defer the hatch well into June. But on most mayfly waters in Ireland and the mildest parts of western Scotland there will usually be steady hatches of mayflies by the last few days of May, and lasting well into June.

Why then is this called the *Mayfly*? On most British and Irish rivers and lakes it is usually much more evident in early June, and there are various different theories about how the name mayfly arose. Can it be because its appearance coincides with the flowering of the may-blossom of the hawthorn? Or might it be connected with the old Julian calendar that was abandoned in 1753, when Parliament adopted the Gregorian system and the date was abruptly changed from the first of September to the twelfth, causing riots in London as the mob panicked and clamoured for Parliament to 'give us back our eleven days!' Under the new dispensation after 1753 the first of June corresponded to the old 22 May, and in those pre-Gregorian days the bulk of the mayfly hatches would indeed have taken place in the month of May. If we reverted to the old calendar, troutfishers who today converge on mayfly waters on, say, 25 May would actually be doing so on 14 May. Might it therefore be more correct to rename this the Junefly? This was a theory sometimes teasingly put forward by one of Ireland's foremost trout flyfishers, A.A. Luce, who was a Senior Fellow of Trinity College, Dublin in the 1960s, when I was a callow freshman who spent too much time fishing and not enough in the library.

As if there were not enough puzzles in the timing of mayfly hatches, there are some waters where the hatch is spread over not merely a couple of weeks but a period of several months. One such is Lough Melvin in County Leitrim, a lough which holds many unexpected puzzles for the fisherman, and where there are sparse hatches of mayflies from late May until as late as August, so that a natural mayfly or a fly-tier's representation may be taken by a trout (and sometimes even by a salmon or a grilse) at any time from spring to late summer.

The final moult from dun to spinner, from subimago to imago, takes place as the insects wait in the shelter of the bankside bushes and trees. Here they change from greendrakes to greydrakes (the females) and blackdrakes (the males), whose genitalia are now exposed and functional for the last act of the drama. Towards late afternoon and then onwards to dusk, the mature spinners fly out from the bushes and flutter high over the water, the lower-flying males and the higher-flying females locating one another by the subtlest pheromone scents. Mating takes place on the wing, and the female needs to mate only once, though certain males will occasionally mate with a succession of females.

There is nothing left for the males to do now except to collapse in final exhaustion and die on or near the water. The females perform the critical final act of depositing their eggs on the water, dipping down and shedding them onto the surface, where they sink to the gravels and marls below and begin the cycle anew. Then the spent females too collapse and die, their usually upright wings now outspread and inert on the water's surface.

Trout become active and begin to feed towards dusk — the fisherman's beloved evening rise — and this coincides with the egg-laying and falling of the spent mayflies, what trout fishers call the fall of spent gnat. These are not as lusciously nutritious as the duns, since the females' loads of eggs have been shed, but trout will feed on them readily, and this is the time when a really big fish may find its way into the landing net. The gathering dusk often sees the largest trout coming on the move, cruising and feeding steadily on the spent gnat, sometimes all through the short spring night. The art — and the dream — of the evening flyfisher is to be able to make an accurate cast and drop a convincing artificial fly into the path of just such a cruising monster.

The Ring-Tail and the Ashen Hawk

Through the rain-spattered side window of the car, made still more opaque by a misting of steam from the wet dogs in the back, the bird seemed at first like a seagull. It rose from the roadside in a swirl of silvery grey, the undersides of its long wings pale against the gloomy sky. Turning on the breeze it swung up and across the line of the road, and then came into clearer view in the swept arcs of the windscreen wipers. There were dark wingtips and a long tail, and as it banked again to our right there was a sudden splash of bright white on the rump. It was a harrier, a mature male hen harrier.

We pulled over into one of the little passing places on the single track road — strictly not to be used unless actually overtaking — and I wound down the window with one hand while the other reached for the binoculars. A gust of wind blasted in through the open window, splashing chill raindrops on my face and across my specs. I cupped my hands and tried to shield the binoculars' object lenses from the heavy droplets as I focussed on the grey shape that was now rowing away purposefully into the wind across a long vista of ploughed heather, where the fine tops of little spruces flickered in the wind on the tops of the peaty ridges.

The hen harrier's very name gives a hint of its reputation, often black and still rather ambiguous today. Dr William Turner, the learned Northumbrian naturalist and fellow of Caius College, Cambridge, listed this raptor in his 1544 account of British birds, the first bird book in English, and proclaimed that 'it gets this name among our countrymen from butchering their fowls'. I often wish they had settled for 'fowl harrier' or somesuch: it can sound awkward and confusing when people speak about 'male hen harriers' or (worse) 'hen hen harriers'.

The confusion is not just one of nomenclature. It is not so very long ago that the male and female were genuinely believed to be birds of quite separate species, the buzzard-brown female looking so very different from her silvery-slatey mate, who is also noticeably smaller and more lightly built. Lots of Victorian ornithological books demonstrate their authors' confusion, and some of the hen harrier's colloquial names in many parts of the British Isles remain unclear even today. In lowland Scotland the ashen-blue male is still often called the Blue Gled, while the female is the Brown Gled; in the west of Ireland the male is variously referred to as the White Kite and the Seagull Hawk; and the terms Brown Hawk and Blue Hawk are widespread — doubly confusing since peregrines (of both sexes) are also commonly called blue hawks. The biologists' *Circus cyaneus* is international, unambiguous and convolutedly dull, and is guaranteed to get you blank looks from most countrymen.

Nature, which opted for marked differences in size and build between male and female in so many species of raptors, really went to town on sexual dimorphism with the hen harrier, adding vivid colour coding to the more usual variation in size. No other British bird exhibits such dramatic differences in coloration, in addition to the usual size and conformation discrepancies found between males and females among diurnal birds of prey. Small wonder, therefore, that it was long believed to be two distinct species, a belief that may still linger. In 1971 I had a long talk about harriers with an elderly retired stalker in Wester Ross, who adamantly maintained that the 'ringtail' and the 'white harrier' were quite different birds, and would not be persuaded otherwise.

Dumfriesshire, where I live, and Galloway and Ayrshire to the west, are harrier country, with mile upon mile of rolling hills, rough marginal land, and extensive commercial conifer forests. It is also an area rich in harrier associations; and a long narrative poem by the Scots poet William Dunbar in 1504, entitled *The False Friar of Tongland* (an abbey in Kirkcudbrightshire), refers to various birds, including the 'Sanct Martynis fowle' — St Martin's bird — which remains the French name for the hen harrier, *le busard Saint Martin*, so called because of the birds' southward wanderings across France in late autumn, around the time of St Martin's Day on 11 November. And in the 1830s it was a Dumfriesshire baronet and laird, Sir William Jardine, who first wrote about the harriers' habit of communal roosting in winter. A generation earlier another Borderer, Dr John Heysham, had shot harriers, and captured young ones, on Newton Common, that has now vanished under the suburbia of Carlisle. He was in no doubt that the brown ringtail and the blueish-white harrier were male and female, having shot both together at the same nest; and he kept live young harriers captive for long enough to witness their moult into adult plumage — good practical observations, although they were made using methods that would land the perpetrator in court nowadays.

The word 'harrier' implies a particular type and style of predation that is distinctly different from what we immediately associate with 'hawk' and 'falcon'. 'Harrier' hints at harrassment, at persistent pursuit, that those other terms don't suggest. And it is a true reflection of the old prejudices against this bird, prejudices that linger and still denote widespread misgivings about the bird and its ways. Watch a hen harrier, or, better still, a pair of hen harriers, hunting on a heathery moor, and you see a methodical questing that is quite unlike the stealthy dash of a sparrowhawk or a goshawk, or the headlong pace and lightning agility of the merlin or the peregrine. Instead the harriers beat along relentlessly in easy, flop-winged flight, skimming low and watchful, quartering their ground with all the methodical steadiness of a pair of pointers or setters. They glide and check and hover and move on and back-track to check again with an effortless, floating, yet deadly purposeful movement. Their measured progress, so tireless and painstaking, makes you think they could miss nothing. There is a particular quality in their hunting style that earned them a place of special prominence in the rogues' gallery of raptors in the old days when every bird with a hooked beak was automatically an enemy of the farmer and the gamekeeper. Perhaps that birddog-like quartering was too similar to the workings of pointers and setters, too clearly a sign that here was a bird that might be a direct competitor for gamebirds, especially partridges and grouse.

The harriers' distinctive flight has caught the eye of many writers about birds. The Scottish ornithologist William Macgillivray wrote in 1837 of 'how beautifully they glide along, in their circling flight, with gentle flaps of their expanded wings, floating, as it were, in the air, their half-spread tails inclined from side to side, as they balance themselves, or alter their course'. Almost three hundred miles away, his contemporary, the Northamptonshire poet, John Clare, described 'a large blue hawk almost as big as a goose. They fly in a swooping manner not much unlike the flight of a heron . . .' and in *The Shepherd's Calendar* (1823) he wrote:

> *A huge blue bird will often swim*
> *Along the wheat when skies grow dim*
> *With clouds — slow as the gales of spring*
> *In motion with dark shadowed wing*
> *Beneath the coming storm it sails*

— a vivid evocation of a male harrier hunting, palely silhouetted against a dark and stormy skyscape.

The brightness of the male's plumage against the darker background of heather or woodland or pasture readily catches the eye, which can be hazardous when you happen to be at the wheel of a car. On the high downland ridges of south Wiltshire I often had harriers flying along close beside the car and parallel to it as I drove to my office at the

Game Conservancy. Winter visitors that annually appeared from November to early March, they were always absorbing to watch, and several times caused me to arrive at my desk later than expected, having pulled in and parked to watch them quartering the huge fields of winter cereals and oilseed rape.

But here, on a west Highland road in mid-March, we were blinking through the rain at what was almost certainly a resident bird, and one that would shortly be nesting not far away. Six weeks later I was back, this time on a bright day of fleeting late-April showers and long periods of chilly sunshine, a steady breeze out of the north-west bringing that special clarity of light that so often accompanies a northerly airstream. To the south of the road there was a wide expanse of open country, a long vista of recently-planted blanket bogland corrugated by the foresters' ploughs, where occasional swathes of unbroken heather and rough grasses had been left undisturbed as firebreaks and rides among the blocks of little trees. The light was perfect, and I could see for miles: and with binoculars and telescope I had a good chance of spotting any harrier activity. I huddled down in the lee of a heathery knoll, and felt suddenly warm. I stabbed my hill crook upright into the soft peat between my legs, extended the telescope and laid it ready beside me, and began to scan with binoculars.

I saw the flash of a white rump, but not of a harrier this time. It was a cock wheatear, erect and alert on a tussock of peat. Then something much larger flickered at the edge of the glasses' field of view, a curlew gliding and calling, then descending on tremulous wings and alighting. A cock grouse called somewhere from the heather above the road and not far behind me, his angry territorial cackle carrying clearly on the breeze. Far off and high above the heathery ridges I could see the jet black silhouette of a single hooded crow, flapping along steadily on one of those solitary corvine point-to-point journeys that presumably originally gave rise to the expression 'as the crow flies'.

Over an hour and a half had passed before I caught sight of the first harrier. It was a male, bright against the background of sombre forestry plough, and about half a mile off, though still clearly to be seen with the binoculars. Steadying the telescope against the hazel shaft of the upright cromach I twisted the eyepiece into crisp focus, and there he was, clear and bright and gliding in a wide circle with only the occasional loose-jointed flap of his wings. He arced and circled again, as if following a familiar course over a favourite piece of country. Then suddenly his flying action changed, and he started to climb, steeply and powerfully. He went up perhaps eighty or ninety feet in a surge of energy, then flipped over and swooped in a steep dive, his pointed, black-tipped wings swept back and slightly folded, almost skimming the tops of the longer heather stalks and the little trees, then bouncing up again in another steep climb. It had a silent energy and grace, but I knew that it was only the distance and the wind direction that prevented me from hearing the harrier's characteristic and incessant chattering calls that accompany the display.

Repeated again and again over his chosen patch of ground, this extended self-advertising skydance was clearly for the benefit of a female somewhere nearby. I swept the area carefully with glasses and telescope, but could not find her. Then the male had gone, and the scene returned to stillness after almost half an hour of this spectacular display.

I lay back in the heather and ate my 'piece', watching for any further signs of harriers on the wing out there across the level bogland. Almost another hour had passed, and I was thinking of moving on, when I heard a squealing cry, the shrill call common to birds of prey, off to my right. I looked round to see the silhouette of a harrier flying quite high, perhaps three hundred yards away. The binoculars confirmed it was a male; but was it the same one? Then there was another burst of shrill chattering, and a second bird flickered into sight, a female this time, her upper parts a warm chocolate-brown, the white splash of her rump vividly contrasting.

She climbed steadily towards the approaching male, who swept over her, and lowered both his bright yellow legs. There was something, small, dark and shapeless, held in his feet. Then he let go of his little burden, which had only dropped a few feet when it was caught by the female, which had flicked over suddenly onto her back and seemed almost to hover for a moment upside down. She righted herself with another twist, less slick and nimble this time, her feet outstretched and grasping her prize, that now seemed to trail a limp wing. Then she set her wings in a deep V, her barred tail slightly fanned out for balance and control, and seemed to parachute gently down among the heathery furrows that lay just out of my sight over a low crest.

The harriers' food pass is dramatic and swift and over in a flash, far quicker than it takes to tell, and it is a sure sign that the pair involved are firmly bonded and have a nesting site not far away. This one was probably among the long heather of the forestry ride just below on my right, perhaps less than a hundred yards off. I couldn't get any closer without the risk of disturbing the birds, and raptors do not react well to disturbance, especially early in their nesting season. So I quietly folded my telescope and slipped away back to the car on the road above, confident of being able to give a pretty precise location to an ornithologist friend who lived not far away, who could check on progress as the spring went by. Back at the car I was greeted by the sight of one very flat tyre; and then a heavy squall began to fling stinging pellets of sleety rain.

The Falcons' Crag

It was early June, and one peregrine eyrie had remained unvisited since I had first been there in late March. The birds there were thoroughly wedded to their cliff site, and they seldom strayed far even in winter, probably because there was plenty of potential prey on hand. The moors that stretched away across the flat plateau behind the cliffs, although they had recently been ploughed for forestry, always held fair numbers of grouse. And the lochs nearby were home to big populations of breeding duck, mainly mallard, and the onset of autumn brought further wildfowl in the form of winter migrants, chiefly teal and wigeon. There were snipe among the rushes and over the boggy fields around the lochs' margins, and woodcock in the fringe of scrubby oaks and birches below the heather line. Even if your name means the wanderer, why wander off to coastal estuaries when there is a rich larder of good winter fare right on your doorstep?

In March these had appeared to be recognisably the same falcons as I had seen there in the previous two seasons, clearly attached to one another and to their perching places, and behaving much the same as ever. They had a good breeding record, the eyrie was tucked away on private land, and I was confident that they would breed successfully once again, so I had not been in any particular hurry to go back and check. But it was a pretty place, one of my favourites, and a friend had invited me for a weekend's fishing on a loch nearby. The mayfly hatch had begun, the trout were taking freely, and there might be a nest of peregrine eyasses to see — the combination was too heady to resist.

A long overnight drive, a late breakfast and a day's fishing passed in quick succession. The day began with a pleasant balmy breeze and occasional glimpses of sun between banks of high cloud. By late morning the cloud had thickened and lowered, the breeze had almost dropped, and it had become warmer. Mayflies were hatching steadily in the little bays, resting on the water after they emerged and waiting for the lacy filligree of their wings to dry, which took longer than usual. A humid atmosphere and no wind slowed the drying process, and the trout were on the move and feeding steadily on the vulnerable insects before they fluttered off to the brief safety of the shore.

By now there was no wind to billow out a dapping line, no wave to animate a team of flies fished as we drifted. We were becalmed, and resorted to single dry flies, casting as accurately as we could into the path of individual feeding trout. Some we simply frightened, others ignored us, a few were hooked and caught — and all the time the cloud cover had become denser and more leaden, the atmosphere muggy and airless. By four o'clock it was almost stiflingly warm and still, and the midges were hatching in their tens of thousands. They found our boat and any exposed areas of our flesh, and there was no hint of any breeze to give us relief from them. Exasperated, we ripped the outboard into life and headed back to the boathouse, glad of the temporary slipstream as it briefly cooled us and blew away the midges' torment. Five nice trout were in the bass of woven rushes as we locked up the boathouse and took down the rods, swatting ineffectually at the clouds of midges and hurrying to get into the sanctuary of the cars.

John had cattle to check, and my thoughts were already ten miles away at the peregrine eyrie. An unexpectedly early end to fishing seemed like a good opportunity to pay it a quick visit, and there might even be a breeze on the hillside to offer relief from the midges and the stuffy humidity. 'We'll expect you for supper about nine', said John, 'And be careful. It feels like thunder is on the way', and off he drove. In a few moments I swung out onto the road and headed westwards towards the distant outline of the hill with its wide apron of young commercial forestry covering its lower slopes.

Twenty minutes later I had pulled in to the locked forestry gates and was scrabbling under the large flat stone where I hoped the padlock key was still kept. It was still there, but muddy and gritty, and needed to be swilled in the roadside stream before I could put it into the lock and open the gate. The gravelly road up through the trees wound and twisted between stands of well-established sitka spruce that stood silent and seemingly lifeless in the stifling air. It is difficult to judge how far you have driven when all the trees look the same and your vision is limited to a narrow gravel track between screens of uniformly dark spruces. But it must have been about three miles before I reached the uppermost fringe of the older trees, and the view opened out to reveal the grey cliffs beyond a rising carpet of younger saplings.

I stopped and switched off the engine, and reached for binoculars and telescope. The whole length of the cliff was in full view from here, and I knew which areas to sweep for a first distant glimpse of the eyrie ledge and the main perching places. A small rowan tree on the clifftop skyline was always my best reference point for locating the eyrie ledge, which was about forty feet below it and a little to the right, under a slightly overhanging outcrop of rock that showed up paler than the rest of that part of the crag. By this stage of the nesting season it and the rocks below should be brightly splashed with the white droppings of the falcons and their chicks, a clear white signal that this was an occupied eyrie, but I needed the binoculars to pick this out in the gloomy light of late afternoon, which now had almost a hint of mist. The roof of the car made a steady rest for the binoculars and the telescope, and there was indeed plenty of whitewash spattering the cliff-face to indicate that the birds were in residence. For ten minutes I waited and watched for any signs of movement, but nothing stirred.

Before I moved any closer I took time to look and listen, and became aware of a steady *churr*-ing sound coming from somewhere down the track. I walked closer and could gradually make out the combined songs of what must have been a dozen or more grasshopper warblers concealed among the small spruce trees. These are furtive and skulking little birds, and seldom easy to see, and here it was like looking for needles in a huge haystack. The acres of little spruces were thickly infested with field rushes and a tangled profusion of brambles, and somewhere among this jungle was a colony of little warblers, all reeling away steadily in their distinctive grasshopper-like way, with a softened but mechanical-sounding note that continued endlessly, now louder, now softer, as the birds turned their heads to and fro, the resulting doppler effect making the *churr*-ing calls appear to rise and fall in tone. Grasshopper warblers are shy and elusive, like so many of the warbler tribe, but this well camouflaged species' fondness for thick cover is combined with a mastery of ventriloquial song, its ratchet-like reeling continuing in endless breathless sessions, yet always difficult to locate and pinpoint accurately. Something in the quality of this steamy air gave the warblers' song an unusual resonance, so that the air itself seemed to pulsate to the birds' continuous calls, as though a dozen flyfishers were simultaneously spinning the ratcheted spools of their fishing reels.

I drove on for another four hundred yards or so, and stopped again where the track swung to the right, following the edge of a tiny loch that the foresters had preserved as a handy source of water in the event of a fire among the trees. It was lightly fringed with long strands of willow moss, reeds and sedges, and there was a pale haze of insects above the water, with countless others steadily hatching in the warm stillness. Everywhere the smooth surface was lightly dimpled with the emergence of insects, and with the larger, rougher rings caused by little trout feeding steadily. Scuttling water-boatmen darted abruptly over the near shallows. In the corner of my eye I glimpsed a movement off to my right, and turned to see a large greyish sedge ploughing a furrowed track across the water, and passing outwards towards the middle of the loch's two or three acres. Suddenly there was a second, following track astern of it in the water, which then bulged and splashed as a bigger trout — a sizeable, keepable trout — rose and engulfed the sedge with a rich sucking plop. There was a rod in the car and dry sedge patterns in my flybox — but no, I had fished enough, and there was a peregrine cliff to check.

Another sweep of the cliff with the telescope still revealed no signs of falcon activity, until I glimpsed a slight movement on the nesting ledge, little more than a hint of something pale that stirred momentarily. An eyass, perhaps; or just the feathers of some fragment of prey moving in the wind? But there was no wind; and the tufts of grass and woodrush up there on the cliff ledges were as motionless as the little trees and rushes around me here on the lower ground. The hope grew that I might just have caught sight of a falcon chick moving on the nest ledge, and such thoughts make the pulse quicken with anticipation.

That big trout was forgotten as I took a further longing look at the ledge, pushed the telescope closed, and started the car's engine again. I drove on and finally parked the car where the track widened out into a turning circle for forestry trucks, at a higher point on the hillside and barely a hundred feet below the falcon's eyrie, and a couple of hundred yards to the left of it. Time for a quick check — telescope slung over my shoulders in its leather case, binoculars around my neck, a notepad and pencils in one jacket pocket, a squeezy bottle of insect repellent and a pipe and tobacco pouch in another.

High above the track and along to my right was a grassy knoll above the mossy scree, a vantage point I had used on previous visits, which gave a clear view down into the eyrie, and this was my objective. Rubber-soled wellies are not ideal hill boots, and definitely not recommended for negotiating moss-grown scree on a clammy day, but I slipped and slithered and grunted my way up to the base of the knoll, pausing to wipe away a torrent of sweat that streamed off my forehead and stung my eyes, before I breathlessly moved into position on the wide grassy top, tufted with woodrush and with bright blood-red points of *cladonia* lichen speckling the fuzz of short grey mosses where the rock was exposed. Flat on my stomach, I inched forwards on my elbows and raised my head to peer over and down towards the ledge.

There was no need for binoculars or telescope to see that this was a successful, occupied eyrie. The young falcons were clearly visible about thirty yards away, and their flat ledge was a mass of feathers and other prey remains. Below the ledge the rocks were thickly smeared with the birds' white droppings, and I could see what looked like other feathered debris from prey littering some of the lower crevices and ledges where it had fallen or been tossed out of the nest.

To get such a close, clear view right into a peregrine eyrie is always a thrill, and I reached for my telescope with the tremulous stealth of a stalker who has just crept up on the stag of his dreams. I inched the tubes out and eased the eyepiece to my right eye, squeezing and twisting the glass to get a clear focus — and there they were. Three well-grown peregrine chicks, rounded and rather shapeless dollops of white down, squatted on the ledge, surrounded by a carpet of feathers and prey scraps. I estimated them to be about four weeks old, and the two that sat near the back of the ledge were already bigger than the third, who squatted about eighteen inches away from them, and tugged gently and repeatedly at what looked like the remains of a duck's wing — almost certainly a male with his two larger and rather sleepy-looking sisters. Of the adult birds there was no sign. Probably away hunting, or perhaps just enjoying the freshness of flight instead of the humid heat of this still air at the cliff face. In this warmth there was no need for the chicks to be brooded or sheltered against the cold, and the two females seemed decidedly dozy. They almost filled the lens of the telescope and their eyes were closed, their heads sunk heavily on their breasts that rose and fell as they breathed in somnolent contentment.

I lay and watched and waited, pausing occasionally to mop my brow and de-mist my specs. The air was so thick with moisture that you might almost have grabbed a fistful and squeezed the water out of it. And no-one who doesn't wear glasses can imagine the frustrations that arise when humidity causes them to steam up, or when a driving drizzle makes them as opaque as the frosted glass on a lavatory window. Perhaps half an hour went by, and still the chicks lay unattended and dozing in the oppressive clamminess of the warm evening air. Then I heard it, clear and unmistakeable — the high *kek-kek-kek*ing call of a peregrine. Just as I glanced upwards from the eyrie ledge and along the cliff face I saw a dark shape flicker out from the crags about two hundred yards away, sickle-shaped wings carrying it upwards in an ascending curve. It was the male, the tiercel of falconers' ancient Norman-French parlance, so-called because he is about a third smaller than the female, the sportsman's true 'falcon'. He had probably been perching there all along, unseen by me, but no doubt quite aware of my car that was parked down the hill in full view. He climbed fast and called again, and an answering falsetto chorus was set up by the three chicks below me, all their sleepiness now replaced by eager expectancy. A third call from another adult peregrine came from high up to my right, and there suddenly was the falcon, flying in heavily and dropping fast towards the cliff, something pale and limp clutched in her feet.

She back-pedalled with flailing wings and landed heavily on the near edge of the eyrie ledge, facing the three noisy chicks and with her back towards me, so that I could not see what she had carried into the nest. She shuffled and seemed to wrestle with her burden, then flapped and rose again, to half-fly, half-jump over her chicks and land on the wider area of rock at the other end of the ledge, her prey still held tightly but only in one foot now. The telescope now gave me a full-frontal close-up as she faced in my direction, and I could see that there was a collared dove in her grasp. The frenzied calls of the clamouring chicks found a counterpoint in the tiercel's *kekk*-ing as he flew back and forth along the cliff, occasionally visible out of the corner of my eye, but mostly well above me as I lay prone and concentrated on the female and her young.

Her dissection of the dove was businesslike and quick, the head half pulled, half cut away by a powerful tugging chop of her toothed bill and flicked to one side; she would probably eat that delicacy herself later. Then she began to pluck and bite deeply into the dove's breast, flicking away tufts of short feathers that slowly drifted down the cliff face in the still air. Then she raised her head with a ragged fragment of flesh in her bill, and with an air of seeming solemnity and intense concentration she offered it with a sideways inclination of her head to the gaping bill of the first of the chicks, one of the larger females that had pushed itself into first place in the feeding queue.

It never fails to impress me with its incongruity, this seeming tenderness and delicacy of a raptor parent towards its young, displayed by a bird that is an accomplished killer by nature and a powerfully intimidating physical specimen. Time and again she braced her clenched feet against the dove's carcase and tore upwards to rip away another morsel of meat, then relaxed from her taut posture and reached gently forward with infinite care to present it accurately into the open bill of one of her beseeching chicks. It took less than ten minutes for her to strip the dove down to little more than a frail mat of bones and feathers, ragged wings outstretched and the sharp keel of its breastbone jutting upwards and deeply notched where the falcon's bill had bitten through it. The excited, shoving urgency of the chicks had subsided now, their movements slower and their high insistent shrieking reduced to an occasional muted call. There is not much meat on a collared

dove, and a good host will serve two per person when giving supper to human guests with healthy appetites. But there had been enough to assuage temporarily the hunger of the three eyasses, before another hunting foray would have to begin, perhaps by the tiercel this time.

Her feeding session ended, the falcon stropped her beak with sweeping sideways movements against the dove's breastbone and her own toes, then slowly fluffed out her feathers porcupine-fashion and shook them in a shuddering shiver, the 'rouse' that falconers interpret as a sign of good health, relaxation and contentment. Each feather then subsided into its place, and the peregrine resumed her usual sleek, alert form. Suddenly she spread her wings and was off on a fast, low flight along the cliff face, finally setting her wings and sweeping up to alight gently on a prominent knob of rock, its top as dark as the feathers of the falcon's back and wings, its lower sides slashed with the chalky white of repeated droppings. Silence and airless stillness possessed the cliff once again.

I took a final look at the eyrie, where the plumply downy eyasses squatted at rest, this time with the young male tucked towards the back of the ledge with one of his sisters, their eyelids drooping, while the other shuffled among the litter of feathers and debris further along the rock, scratching and pulling in a desultory way at a pinkish piece of bone. It was now just after 7.30 p.m., and time to go. I wriggled back from my observation place on top of the knoll, and clicked the three tubes of the telescope closed and back into their leather case. Again I fumbled and slithered on the mossy rocks and steep grass that led down to the base of the cliff. Once there, I raised my binoculars and looked up at the falcon's rocky perch. She was still there, motionless, with her head pulled back into her shoulders so that she seemed quite neckless, and total indifferent to my presence, which she could not have missed. I walked steadily and unhesitatingly back to the car, hoping she would not be prompted into a display of angry, noisy defensiveness, but nothing happened. A final glance from the car showed her still to be hunched and statuesque on her upthrust tooth of rock, and there was neither sight nor sound of the tiercel. Perhaps he was indeed hunting somewhere; or perhaps just perching, inconspicuous and still, like his mate.

The warm heaviness of the air finally collapsed into a crashing thunderstorm as I was driving back along the track between the spruces, the furious rain lashing the windscreen into an opaque film despite the wipers' fastest speed, the torrent of heavy drops churning up muddy splashes on the forest road where there had been a thin scattering of fine summer dust. The fire-dam lochan was churned into a grey expanse of spiky splashes by pellets of damp hailstones, and the thunder crashed overhead. My final thoughts were to imagine the falcon sweeping back along the cliff to shelter and brood her chicks against the storm, her sleek slate-blue feathers better suited to shed heavy rain and hailstones than their light down.

The rain had stopped when I got out to unlock the forest gate, and already there was a sharp line of brighter sky off in the distance beyond the falcons' cliffs. The air was fresher and cooler, rinsed clear by the storm that was rumbling its way off towards the east. A week later my friend the local vet telephoned me to report that he had been up to the cliff and had ringed the three eyasses, which were all fit and strong, and now close to fledging.

It seems incredible that peregrines should now be so successful and numerous, when barely twenty years ago their very survival as a species seemed to be at risk. Ironically, it all began with complaints by racing pigeon enthusiasts about excessive losses of valuable pigeons to peregrines. (In view of the amazing numbers of pigeon rings I have found in certain eyries, I am not really surprised; and in wartime the government had authorised the shooting of peregrines in an attempt to minimise losses of homing pigeons carrying military messages.) Controversy over peregrine numbers and pigeon mortality led to the first systematic post-war survey of falcon numbers in Britain, and the outcome caused consternation among ornithologists and conservationists. Instead of being so numerous as to constitute a hazard to racing pigeons, peregrines were found to be in dire straits, their numbers tumbling towards extinction.

In just a few years, civilised man's pollution had done what generations of over-zealous gamekeepers and government sponsored extermination pro-grammes during two world wars had failed to do, slashing peregrine numbers because of the insidious effects of persistent environmental poisons, especially those derived from the use of DDT, mercurial seed dressings, and PCBs which are by-products of many industrial processes. Their eggshells became thinned to the point where the eggs became too fragile for the birds to incubate them, the adults' fertility dropped, and many peregrines that did not die directly as a consequence of the toxins developed strange behavioural abnormalities. The falcons disappeared almost totally from the coastal cliffs of southern England, where many eyries had been occupied continuously for centuries, and the decline was echoed in almost every corner of the British Isles, and in Europe and across North America. Those of us who made the annual rounds of the eyries in spring in the late 1960s thought that we might merely be charting the peregrines' unstoppable slide towards oblivion. The once-ubiquitous sparrowhawk seemed to be sharing the same fate, its numbers in rapid decline across much of Britain.

But the outcome was a wonderful affirmation of the recuperative powers of these species. The toxins were banned, the environment became cleaner, and the peregrine was no longer at the head of a food-chain of contaminated birds, steadily building up residues of poisons in their fat. The decline slowed and stopped, the numbers of successful breeding pairs began to increase, and by the 1980s it was clear that recovery had been total. Better than that, the falcons were seen to become more numerous than at any recent period, with the British breeding population passing the 1,000 pairs mark. With few exceptions, the old eyries were all re-occupied, and peregrines steadily colonised newly-created nesting sites in quarries and even on high buildings. In May 1993 a pair of peregrines actually nested and laid eggs on a disused gasometer in Dublin, presumably because all the traditional nesting sites in the nearby Dublin mountains and Wicklow were already occupied, and this brought an abrupt halt to a demolition gang's plans to knock it down. Such an event would have been the stuff of dreams back in 1970, when I used to visit innumerable empty or unsuccessful peregrine eyries in the hills south of Dublin. Now the sparrowhawks have bounced back, too, and are now probably as common as ever in their accustomed habitats of wooded farmland across the British Isles. It is rare for a day to pass here in the south of Scotland without Judy or myself seeing a wild sparrowhawk somewhere close to the house.

Another irony that emerged from the same critical period was the development of successful techniques for the captive breeding of birds of prey, formerly thought to be virtually impossible. Not surprisingly, it was the practising falconers of Europe and America who led the way when they saw their beloved wild raptors at risk. By 1990 it had become common practice for British falconers to breed almost every species of raptor in captivity, thereby not only securing for themselves a future supply of birds for falconry, but also showing how captive raptors can form a strategic reserve as a hedge against catastrophe striking the wild birds. Countless thousands of captive-bred birds of prey have been released into the wild by falconers in western countries, a practical contribution to raptor conservation that no other group of people would have had the expertise or enthusiasm to achieve.

The peregrine is the *peregrinator*, the *pelerin*, the wanderer. Though some, like the pair on that western crag, seldom move far because ample prey is available nearby throughout the year, many others forsake their summer breeding haunts, drifting off in autumn to the lowlands, the river estuaries and the coast. There, duck and waterfowl of many kinds are their staple winter quarry. With a team of friends I regularly visit a small ornamental loch in the Annan valley, and it is quite common to see one and sometimes two falcons in the vicinity, following the teal and pochard that come in off the Solway, and no doubt also attracted by the resident mallard. One November evening of gales and scudding grey skies we went to see the birds that the storm had driven inland, and among them was a peregrine tiercel. I first saw him, a mature bird in slatey-blue plumage, perched in the top of an old Scots pine on an island in the loch, a perfect vantage point from which to see the ducks that zipped and tumbled around as dusk gathered.

At the first sight of us he spread his wings quite calmly and sailed up in an effortless spiralling flight, levelling out several hundred feet above the loch and then circling steadily to watch all that went on below. Little parties of teal kept sweeping in up the valley, travelling low and fast with the westerly wind behind them, and three times we saw him make a long passing feint at them, more for the fun of it than in earnest, it seemed. He knew we were there, crouched in the partial concealment of the old butts of sculpted rhododendrons, but had no qualms about repeatedly passing close to us — a trusting act that would probably have been his last in the bad old days when everything with a hooked beak was shot. I watched in admiration, and then a streaking group of wild mallard hurtled by, and the tiercel set his wings and stooped in anger this time, a blisteringly-fast dive with wings tucked back in the way that designers of variable-geometry fighter aircraft try to emulate. I spun round and tried to follow the flight of quarry and hunter, but both were lost to sight behind the riverside trees, and the conclusion was unseen. But the determined, near vertical stoop of a mature peregrine is so awesome and purposeful that it seems nothing could escape.

Peregrines and merlins are common sights in winter along the Solway littoral of marshes and pastures. No-one who has not seen it can imagine the blind panic and terror that a hunting falcon creates among wading birds. They can ignore a raptor that simply perches and constitutes no immediate threat; but they instinctively know when a falcon is hunting in earnest, and then the air is instantly filled with wheeling, screaming, tumbling masses of wings, a chaotic fleeing and manoeuvring in terrified unison, the redshank and dunlin and plover and knot seeking individual safety in their collective evasive jinkings and dodgings, all designed to confuse the pursuing falcon. Alone, a solitary bird might be cut down at the first stoop; but these frenzied group responses enhance each individual's chances of escape. But the clear symptoms of utter panic and shieking terror are what strike the onlooker, prompting us to reflect that here is a degree of natural fear and horror far beyond anything that mankind can contrive to inflict upon wildlife, yet enacted continually whenever hunting falcons and their fleeing prey meet on the bleak estuaries and the winter marshes.

The Goat of the Air

The low whitewashed house has two outlooks, utterly different and wholly complementary. Eastwards there is nothing but sea, grey or blue or slate-black by turns in the changing lights, with the Mull of Kintyre and the further silhouettes of Islay and the Paps of Jura, purplish-dark on the horizon. (Seeing that view often reminds me of the glorious Irishism — perpetrated by a Welshman — about views across the Irish Sea. The chronicler Gerald of Wales visited Ireland in 1183 and wrote about his visit, remarking that 'Ireland can often be seen clearly from Britain, but from Ireland it is difficult to see Britain *because of the distance*!') From the seaward side of the house we have to stand on tiptoe and strain to look downwards before we can glimpse the tumbling slope of gorse that cascades to the narrow fringe of green fields dotted with the white blobs of sheep, lying between the hills and the sea.

Westwards, a slightly rising slope leads the eye to a long sweep of level heather, grasses and rushes. Beyond and just below the crest of the skyline lie miles of rough and level moorland, the haunt of buzzard and raven, curlew and hen harrier, the rare grouse and the wandering herds of feral goats. Deep glens penetrate back into the high land, and along their sides extends a winding apron of gentler land, a fringe of little farms below the heather line, with sheep and dairy cattle enfolded in the small fields between high hedges of hawthorn punctuated with ash trees and occasional contorted oaks.

Not many places I know offer such wild variety, a compact vertical arrangement of habitats that rises from seashore and coastal crags through low farmland, scarp cliffs and high and rolling heather moorland in less than a mile from the sea. From the door I can set off with the dogs and traverse a few hundred yards of sheep-nibbled pasture alive with curlews, wheatears and skylarks in spring, and riddled with the honeycombed excavations of rabbits, and have the setter quartering on wide sweeps of heather within five minutes of setting out.

This early July evening she was laid up, nursing a sore toe after two long days of grouse-counting on a moor a few miles away to the south. Hours of pounding with that deceptively effortless loping gallop had taken their toll, and although she was as eager as ever to go with me, her tail lashing in anticipation, she carried a hind leg tucked up underneath her. It was best to leave her to rest and recover, protesting and forsaken-looking though she was. Instead, the old labrador bitch fussed and fretted around me as I pulled on my boots, her fleshy otter's tail flailing against my legs, as she realised that she alone was to go with me.

Over the grassy field pock-marked by rabbits her head went down and her black, wet nose searched for some hot and recent scent to follow. A flash of a white scut from a clump of thistles sent her racing after a rabbit, which made it safely to the burrow inches ahead of her. Only September and the annual onset of yet another early autumn myxomatosis outbreak would slow them enough for her chases to be successful, but she lives in eternal hope. Over the first stone wall and onto sheep pasture, she closed in to heel and followed in my shadow; for I had taught her that it was important not only not to chase sheep, but to be clearly *seen* not to chase them. If any of my farmer neighbours happened to be watching, they would be sure to approve of her behaviour.

It was still and warm, with a hint of distant thunder in the air. The previous two days had been hot and dry, followed just before dawn by a sudden thunderstorm that had passed quickly, leaving a long spell of soaking rain in its wake. By late morning it had stopped raining, and now the air was warm and heavy with moisture. Rainsoaked grass and rushes and flowers and all the vegetation made the air rich with sappy scents. And if these were so apparent to me, how much more they must have meant to a dog, with its infinitely sophisticated sense of smell, after days of hot and dusty weather, when all scents had been burnt away as the rising sun hit the last of the overnight dew.

By the edge of the far field I sat down on a heap of tumbled stones by the wall, and looked down at the circling cruciform shapes of the fulmars as they swirled and glided on wooden-stiff wings, to the sounds of satisfied gruntings and chucklings of many others that perched below me on ledges in the cliff. The steady updraught buoyed them up on their ceaseless soarings and swoopings. Beyond, where the line of cliffs turned out of sight, there were kittiwakes and a solitary buzzard that hung in the uprush of air and circled tightly on moth-like motionless wings.

Off to my left, inland from the cliff edge, a succession of small fields led down a gentle slope towards a hollow of abandoned grassland. There the spiky field-rushes had taken over, and beyond was a long vista of straggly heather dotted with a few small boggy pools, their mirror-flat surfaces reflecting a sky of pale grey. A few duck had nested there earlier in the year, and herons came drifting in occasionally from the big heronry in the high beeches of the castle parkland just over the skyline. The old dog knew from experience that there were usually a few hares here, too, crouched in the drier tussocks and ready to jump up at our feet, to take her on a headlong dash across the plashy acres of mosses and heathery bogland. What dog can resist the sight and scent of a hare, a scent that drives them into ecstacies of single-minded hunting, a dashing streak of reddish-brown that has them pelting off in mad pursuit? Twice she chased and failed, chased and failed, returning to my side with heaving flanks, her tongue panting in a froth of exertion.

Below the gentle slope and just this side of the heathery bog there was the remains of an old dry-stone wall, its boulders tumbled onto the emerald grass or precariously askew on other slipping slabs of dark grey. A tangle of gorse and hawthorn and rushes had encroached among the gaps in the old field dyke. Another rabbit bolted from a tuft of reeds and thistles into the shelter of a pile of stones, but there was no chasing this time, not even a hint of a pursuit. The dog had expended her first surge of energy and simply stood by my side, eyes blazing and ears cocked.

Where a gnarled thorn bush had tilted sideways, defeated by the unremitting winds off the sea, I found a raised mound of short grass and dry earth. I swept away a scattering of pelletted rabbit droppings and sat down, my back against the stem of the wind-thrown thorn, my view a wide arc of damp bogland, heather and rushes. The labrador crept close, turned in a series of tight circles, and curled up against my left thigh, the damp warmth of her coat soaking through the light tweed of my breeks.

We waited, me alert and she now deeply asleep. A rabbit lolloped past within a few inches of my boots, up the line of the ruined wall, to disappear among the stones with a vivid flick of scut and a flurry of hind legs. Far away beyond the heathery slope a dark figure strode up a green field beyond the little road, a white plastic sack of feed thrown over his shoulder, and a flock of sheep converged on him, their distant calls audible as he shook the bag's contents into a series of small feeding troughs.

Mingling with the far noise of the sheep there came a tremulous bleating, like a goat calling. It throbbed and died away, and suddenly I was alert and watching, despite the drowsy softness of the early evening air. This was what I had come to find. Again it came, throbbing and thrumming in a shimmering wave of short-lived sound, like a fiddle string bowed gently with a shivering and resonant *tremolo*, the vibrant sound of a drumming snipe.

There followed a fumbling search in my pockets for the little pair of binoculars amongst a tangle of corded straps and lens covers before I could bring them to bear on the level greyness of the sky above the heather. Then there was a fuzzy dark shape, then another twist of the focussing ring, then a clear image of a small bird that flew level, before tipping forward into an arrowing dive. The thrumming, quavering sound came again for a few seconds, then seemed to be cut off suddenly, leaving nothing but the distant sounds of the feeding sheep and lambs, and the rhythmic sigh of the dog's breathing at my side.

Again and again it bleated, as the bird climbed and levelled off and swooped again, like a dark and stylised arrowhead against the leaden sky. There was a finely-pointed bill thrust out like a long needle in front of a slender head, and the bird's body seemed like a narrow lance, both wings swept back like curved barbs. Behind them was a stubby tail slightly flared out like a narrow dark wedge, and from both its edges there extended the outermost tail feathers, like two fine additional barbs on this self-propelled aerial harpoon.

This is a Celtic landscape, littered with the remains of tumuli and stone circles and menhirs. The ancient peoples who lived here must have seen and heard the snipe too, soaring and diving over the sodden peatlands with this plaintive, insistent sound that is repeated again and again on the warm air of late spring and summer. In Gaelic it is *gabhar a-thair*, 'the goat of the air', or *meann-an-athair*, 'the kid of the air'; and in the old Teutonic language of ancient Britain and Scandinavia it is *haeferblaete*, the 'goat-bleater', so similar to the vernacular 'heather bleater' by which it is still known in parts of northern Scotland and north-western Ireland. In Welsh it is *gafr-y-gors*, 'the goat of the marshes', or *dafad-y-gors*, 'the sheep of the marshes'.

In a dozen other languages all across northern and western Europe there occur similar names with similar meanings, 'the bog bleater', 'the little goat of the bogs', the 'bleating kid of the marshes', 'the goat of the air', 'the bleater that flies', 'the goat of the half-light'. Before the current Latin term *gallinago* was chosen by taxonomists to signify the true snipe species, their Latin name was *capella*, 'the little she-goat', which was a good way of incorporating the innumerable vernacular names for snipe in its formal designation. What a pity it is now *gallinago*, for there is nothing gallinaceous about this wild marshland wader. (Many other European countries have names for snipe that do not fasten on this unique breeding season sound, but instead emphasise the bird's most prominent physical feature, its long pointed bill — the French *bécassine*, the German *schnepfe*, the Russian *békas*, the Portuguese *narseja*. The ancient English words *snyte* and *snype* are closely linked to nose-associated words like snout and snuff and snuffle, and also to neb, often used to mean bill or beak.)

The bleating sound of breeding snipe on the wing gave rise to a wealth of folklore and legends: for more serious-minded ornithologists there raged a controversy about how the sound was created. Was it vocal? Or did the bird generate this distinctive sound by some mechanical means, such as the rushing of air through its feathers? German and Polish experts inclined to the mechanical theory, and even had whole snipe stuffed and mounted in the drumming attitude, where a current of air was blown across them and was said to be able to generate the distinctive bleating sound. Others claimed to have heard snipe bleating while settled on the nest; and so the controversy rumbled on, until Sir Philip Manson-Bahr of Cambridge and Eric Parker, editor of *The Field*, clinched the matter in the 1930s by affixing a snipe's two stiff outer tail feathers to arrows shot into the air, and to a cork whirled around on a string, and thereby created the winnowing sound of a displaying snipe by the vibration of the feathers at a critical speed of just over twenty miles per hour.

And so I watched this bird above the plashy little wilderness of heather, sphagnum and hill grasses, as it climbed and dived and drummed, its sound lasting barely two seconds each time before the bird levelled out and climbed again. The humid air seemed to amplify and enhance the sound's resonance that pulsated and throbbed again and again, briefly and insistently, with an almost physical force. Drumming is attributed almost solely to the male birds, though a perceptive friend of mine promptly inquired why then do the females have the same stiff outer tail feathers. Another retorted, equally promptly, that it was probably for the same reason as human males have nipples — i.e. for no good reason! So this was almost certainly a displaying male, and somewhere amid the tussocks and little pools and rushy clumps there would be a nest and a discreetly-hidden female. I nudged the dozing dog into life again, and we slipped away, returning the way we had come, past the still circling fulmars and over the pastures, to the almost stifling warmth of a kitchen where the cooking of supper made the moist air still more unbearably hot and sticky. At last light another thunderstorm broke, its jagged flashings followed by a deluge of heavy rain. This time it left the night air fresh and clear, with the silver pinpoints of the stars showing brightly overhead.

Three weeks later I went back the same way, this time on a fresh day of cool breeze and high cumulus clouds. There was a scattering of young rabbits almost everywhere I looked, and keeping an eager dog to heel took more than mere verbal discipline. This time it was the setter, trotting by my side on a lead, and not released until we had traversed the rabbity pastures and reached the boggy heather. There I slipped off the lead and cast the dog out across the wind. Her first two or three sweeps settled her into that steady galloping pace that a fit bird-dog can maintain almost endlessly, and she even managed totally to ignore a hare that sprang up almost under her feet, a demonstration of steadiness that would have won her plaudits at a field trial. Then she faltered and slowed and stopped, her head held high and turned directly into the eye of the wind as she subsided gently into a low crouch.

It took me a few minutes to pick my way across the rank heather and the sphagnum pools to reach her, and I slipped the rope lead back over her head. I held her beside me and waited, watching the ground ahead of us carefully. Then a snipe rose, with a dry *scaape*-ing cry, flickering low over the heather and then climbing suddenly and circling back over us, calling again and again, and mounting higher in a spiralling flight. With luck, we had found the nest. Keeping the dog close by my side we rose gently and made our way off to the left, towards a low ridge of grass which marked the line of a tumbled and overgrown stone wall about a hundred yards from the spot where the snipe had risen. There we crossed over the low hummock of turf and rocks, and crouched down as low as possible behind it. I took a turn of the setter's lead around my leg, to leave my hands free and allow me to reach for the telescope that was slung in its leather case over my hip.

The snipe had continued to circle high overhead, mostly silent as we had made our withdrawal, and then I saw it suddenly flicker down and land back in the grassy heather close to the place where it had risen. I took a careful line on the spot and trained the telescope on it, and then simply watched and waited. The image in the glass encompassed a circle of ground perhaps twenty feet across, and every strand of rough grass and tuft of heather could be seen clearly in the bright light conditions. I had a good chance of seeing any bird that moved within that little circle of ground.

After a few minutes I got accustomed to the flickering movements of grass and heather as it moved in the breeze, and then I caught a hint of another movement, something that I could not quite distinguish, but that was different from the wind-tossing of the vegetation. I waited and watched, and then I saw it again, clearer this time, the head and long bill of a snipe. In the crisp focus of the lens I could see its dark eye shining like a tiny black berry. Then it moved again, out from among the heather stalks and onto an open patch of short mossy grass. There were two small shapes by the bird's side, two rounded forms that looked like large bumble bees. Two snipe chicks and one of their parents — and almost certainly the male adult, too.

Snipe eggs, typically four in a clutch, do not hatch simultaneously; in the ornithologists' technical terminology they are 'asynchronous hatchers'. And that is where the male plays an important part in the process of caring for the young chicks. After the eggs have been laid and incubation has begun, the male snipe tends to hand over most of the nesting duties to the female, and he may then spend a good deal of his time living apart from her, perhaps displaying alone at some distance from the nest. But when hatching time approaches he is usually back at the nest, perhaps summoned by the high-pitched calls of the chicks inside the eggs, and it is quite common for him to take the first one or two chicks under his wing, brooding and caring for them while the female remains to attend the remaining eggs as they hatch.

Incubation and hatching are furtive and secretive times, and the birds' need for security and concealment is helped by the cryptic camouflage of their plumage, subtly streaked and shaded to elude all but the sharpest eyes of a hunting raptor — or a searching birdwatcher — and by the birds' extraordinary ability to suppress almost all their body scent at this critical time of year. Scent is a sensory dimension in which human beings can only participate when it is at its most gross and obvious, as with foxes and wild goats, but the infinitely sensitive nose of a dog can be our ally. And even they may encounter problems when the birds' natural hormonal mechanisms subdue their customary scents to almost nil, as a protection against hunting foxes and other predatory mammals.

A female snipe on her eggs seems almost to emit no scent at all, to judge by the number of times I have stumbled upon nests that have been missed by my dogs, experienced bird-dogs that would ordinarily never miss a point on a squatting snipe or fail to retrieve a fallen bird. I have walked over unattended snipe chicks, tiny and still damp after hatching, and had my dogs show no signs of detecting any scent whatever. Yet on other occasions I have had pointers and setters, and even a steady old labrador, wind and locate an adult snipe and chicks, when the weather has been just right for good scent; and I suspect that a male snipe may emit a much stronger scent than his partner, so making it easier for dogs to locate them and their early-hatched chicks than to find the female and her eggs or recently-hatched young.

Birds of the Hills,
Birds of the Heath

Spring comes late to the high hills of Britain, and simple logic might tempt us to think that birds' nesting times will therefore begin late too, to make the most of the better and slightly more reliable weather of the later spring months. But since Britain enjoys changeable and sometimes wildly unpredictable weather, as distinct from a settled climate, it is perfectly possible to have a heavy fall of snow in May, as happened as these words were being written in mid-May 1993. A sudden cold snap brought a fall of more than six inches of snow to ground above 600 feet from Lancashire northwards, and from our kitchen windows at just 400 feet we could clearly see a blanket of snow on the higher pastures to the north across the valley. It was a wet and clinging layer that vanished within thirty-six hours, but it was sufficient to bring disaster to the earliest broods of tiny grouse chicks, and caused a high proportion of hen grouse to abandon eggs that were virtually on the point of hatching. Within a couple of days the hill keepers had seen the extent of the damage that had occurred, and many moors were rapidly revising their shooting plans, and in some cases cancelling their August and September shooting altogether.

Game and wildlife management in the hills is always at the mercy of the weather, and a bad season can mean the loss of most of all essential revenue. No shooting means no income from shooting, and the moor owner has to dig deeper into his personal financial reserves if he is to retain the estate staff whose work is essential to the continuing maintenance of heather moorland habitat, and to the many species of birds and mammals and plants that share it with the grouse. Add to this Scotland's additional burden of sporting rates, levied on average bag returns from earlier years, that have to be paid as a first charge on the land, even if not a single shot is fired, nor a solitary penny received by way of sporting income during that season, and it becomes clear that upland ownership is a matter of small and uncertain returns and continual injections of more funds.

How ironic, therefore, to realise that Britain's wild heather uplands, unique in Europe, and treasured by sportsmen and naturalists alike, attract not one penny of grant aid or other public support. To secure the future of these glorious hill habitats and their wildlife, they need at least the same financial incentives and support as intensive hill farming and forestry, activities which have both done so much environmental damage to the sensitive ecology of Britain's high, wild and lonely places.

It was not only grouse that paid the price of that unseasonable May snowfall. To the west, in Galloway, one hill sheep farmer lost almost half of his flock of 250 ewes, killed by the sudden chill of the wet snow within less than a day of having been shorn of their heavy spring fleeces. Hill land that may be a comfortable vista of sunny slopes swept by the shadows of light clouds and alive with the bubbling cries of curlews and the *chack*-ing of wheatears one day may see dawn break on thick snow and hard frost the next morning. Hill birds simply cannot count on the coming of reliable weather before they begin nesting, and so their breeding cycle often begins early, sometimes well before the last of winter has retreated.

Like the raven and the peregrine, the golden eagle starts to nest early in the year. Territories are held from year to year, and are more widely spaced than those of any other British bird of prey, since a pair of these massive birds needs a wide swathe of hill land over which to hunt if they are to find sufficient winter food for survival, and to glean enough spring prey to feed themselves and their young. Densities of breeding pairs are highest in the Western Highlands, where sheep carrion is readily available, but breeding success is highest in the Eastern Highlands where live prey in the form of grouse, ptarmigan and hares is much more abundant.

Eagle numbers in Scotland gradually dwindled in the nineteenth century, and the species became extinct in Ireland and England, but some recovery followed the Highland Clearances, when large-scale human population movements were followed by vastly increased numbers of sheep and deer, and thus an increased supply of carrion in areas that were less disturbed by human activity than formerly. The human tragedy of those grim clearances had some unexpected benefits for Britain's largest bird of prey, and the reduction in the numbers of gamekeepers during two world wars probably helped them, too.

By the 1950s, however, the eagle population was under renewed pressure in the aftermath of the myxomatosis epidemic, which wiped out the ubiquitous rabbit and thereby removed an important prey species. And by the 1960s the outlook for Britain's eagles was bleak, with an estimated 150 pairs confined to the Highlands and Islands and Galloway, as the pernicious and lingering toxins of sheep-dips containing dieldrin, lindane and DDT threatened their ability to survive and breed to secure their future. But the banning of the worst environmental contamination brought the same swift recovery as for other raptors, and by the end of the 1980s the Scottish population was estimated at well over 400 pairs, higher than at any time since the early 1800s. The English Lake District was also recolonised by at least one breeding pair from the 1970s onwards, their well-guarded eyrie visible from an RSPB viewing point at Haweswater.

In Wester Ross the soaring peaks and jagged ridges of ancient Torridonian sandstone were shrouded in a dusting of snow as I went out with the stalkers for one of the final red deer culling days in mid-February. There was a steely gleam from crags where the frost had clamped its grip on waterfalls and turned them into walls of ice, and the still air held a bone-chilling coldness that gave no hint of any end to the long northern winter. We had trudged almost six miles up the glen, the garron's breath steaming like a furnace as it plodded along with the deer-saddle harness creaking rhythmically, when we heard a shrill barking call from high overhead. An eagle sailed across the valley, high above us and giving only an occasional leisurely flap of its massive wings, set on a steady course for a line of sheer cliffs to the north. It was a well-established nesting cliff, that had been in use for as long as seventy-year-old Johnnie MacDonald could remember. His father, the estate's head stalker before him, had first shown him the eagles' nest as a six-year-old boy, whose little legs had been unable to contend with the long miles of rough hill track, so he had been led there, perched proudly on the pony's deer saddle.

We paused to tether the garron to the hitching pole, a five-foot length of stout larch that had been stripped of bark and polished to a deep patina by years of deer rubbing against it to ease their itching coats and clean their antlers in late summer. Johnnie rubbed a plug of tobacco between gnarled hands and lit his pipe with care, placing a perforated silver cap over the glowing bowl so that the black twist did not burn too hot or fast in the hill air. 'Watch him, now, and ye'll likely see him land on the ledge they're using this year' — and three telescopes were steadied on cromachs and trained on the receding bird. As it neared the cliff, the eagle seemed to pause and back-pedal with its wings, slowing to stalling speed and dropping in slow motion onto a rocky platform with wings upstretched high above its back.

'That must be the one they're going to use this year, same as last spring,' muttered Johnnie as his teeth clenched the pipe-stem and he lay back in the heather and braced his stalking glass against his stick. 'There are two more nesting ledges just around the corner of that outcrop, but they haven't used them for a year or two. It was from one of those that my grandfather shot the two adults and took both eaglets from the nest for his lordship, and he had them stuffed in Inverness.' I remembered the huge glass case I had seen in the lodge gunroom, with the two mature eagles and their downy young set up as a montage on a papier-mache base painted to look like lichened rock; skilful work from the golden age of Victorian taxidermy, and a sad reminder of the old attitudes to birds with hooked beaks.

Telescopes were snapped shut and returned to their leather cases as we moved on, for the daylight hours were short and precious, and there was a hind cull to complete. But in the afternoon, as we led the pony down the glen with its burden of two hinds lashed to the saddle, we paused for a final look, and saw another eagle, bigger this time, sailing in with a sizeable branch in its grasp. The female was refurbishing her eyrie, that already contained enough accumulated sticks from past seasons to make a sizeable bonfire.

I was back in the glen in late July, on a sultry day when only the exposed ridges and the high tops enjoyed a hint of breeze and gave relief from the clouds of midges. It was the day after old Johnnie's funeral, when a packed church full of stalkers and shepherds and landowners was a testimony to the respect he had enjoyed among the neighbouring glens. These men had gathered sheep with him year after year, had learned their craft as stalkers, and had shot their first stags under his stern but wise tutelage. His two sons had been with him on that last day, when he had bent down to take a drink from the burn and fallen gently forward and lain still in the grass and heather, his heart suddenly stilled among the hills where he had so often walked young, fit men to a standstill, the blue fumes from that reeking pipe almost seeming to help propel him up the steepest slopes.

Across the deep valley the telescope gave me a clear view down into the eagles' eyrie, the untidy platform of rock and sticks now bedecked with fresh green strands of woodrush which eagles, and buzzards too, like to bring in to decorate their nests. One well-grown eaglet lay prone amidst a jumble of ragged prey remains, basking in the heat. Young Johnnie, now head stalker in his father's place, had told me they had laid two eggs, and while out ear-tagging young deer calves on the hill he had seen that both had hatched successfully. But now there was only one youngster to be seen, presumably a sign that the usual Cain-and-Abel sibling strife had been concluded in favour of the older and stronger chick, which often manages to hog the food and starve and bully its companion to death, finally to be pushed out of the nest.

For over two hours I waited and watched, content to enjoy the fresh warmth of the mountain heights and look out for the return of one of the adult eagles. But neither appeared, and the young eaglet still lay in swooning contentment on its warm ledge with a larder of prey within easy reach if it should feel peckish. Then it was time to move on, to follow the line of the climbers' ridge walk westwards to where I would drop back into the valley and take the path down to where the car was parked. There were snow buntings among the stony outcrops, sturdy little finches that called clearly from their rocky perches and moved in a flickering of black and white along the crags, and I disturbed several small groups of hinds and yearlings that were seeking respite from the torment of summer flies in the coolness of the highest corries.

On these western deer forests grouse are not especially encouraged, although there are always a few

coveys on the low ground. This is wet, poor hill land with only patchy heather where grouse have always been sparse, and on the main stalking beats they are usually unwelcome, and actively discouraged. An unexpected covey of grouse exploding from the heather as you creep in to take a shot is a sure alarm to the deer, leaving only a glimpse of pale rumps and dun shapes scattering at a gallop, with a disappointed rifle and an exasperated stalker left defeated and downcast. But in any case these high and stony places in the corries and along the ridges above two thousand feet are well above the grouse line, too bare and devoid of heather to provide the food and shelter that are so essential.

This is not the haunt of the red grouse, but its cousin the ptarmigan, *Lagopus mutus*, the 'changeable grouse', as its formal name suggests. The British subspecies, which for two centuries has been confined to the highest hills of Scotland, is additionally labelled *millaisi*, in recognition of the careful studies of Highland ptarmigan carried out by Sir John Guille Millais, one of the most distinguished late Victorian ornithologists, sportsmen and wildlife artists, and son of the Pre-Raphaelite painter Sir John Everett Millais.

In winter a pure snowy white, relieved only by red wattles, a black eye stripe and black tips to the tail feathers, the ptarmigan's summer plumage is a subtle mottling of sandy-buffs with a delicate tracery of vermiculated greys and creams, that gives it perfect camouflage when it crouches among the lichens and tumbled rocks of the high hills. I was within a mile of the end of the high ridge walk when I glimpsed a movement among the stony rubble ahead of me, something that moved and stopped and moved off again. I paused and watched and nothing happened, but as I walked forwards again there was another abrupt scampering, and suddenly three or four ptarmigan heads were silhouetted clearly, like a cluster of little golf club heads. Again I took a few steps forwards, and this time the heads sank slowly out of sight, and then the air was suddenly full of flickering wings that gleamed purest white in the bright mountain light.

The covey sped forwards and then swung to the right, sweeping out over the dizzying slopes that fell away to the glen below, flying in close formation with a bright twinkling of silvery wingtips, and banking again to swing round almost below me. Lost from sight momentarily below a bare outcrop, they swung into view again, climbing this time and now breasting the ridge ahead of me. In unison they raised their wings and dipped their tails and pitched down with a final fluster of wingbeats onto the bare rocky expanse about three hundred yards ahead, dipping their heads low and scuttling immediately for the cover of a patch of stones and boulders. My binoculars allowed me to see them tuck themselves away, each bird finding its individual hiding place, yet all remaining within just a few yards of one another. I walked on along the ridge towards them, and was within less than twenty yards before they moved off again, not taking wing or even seeming particularly concerned by my arrival, but scampering steadily ahead of me among the rocks with something of the confiding familiarity of domestic poultry. Here on the high tops man is an unfamiliar and infrequent intruder, the eagles and peregrines and the wandering hill foxes holding greater daily terrors for these rarest and most specialised of our gamebirds, that cling like ice-age relics to the highest, coldest and barest places on our northern hills, relying only on their cryptically camouflaged plumage, their eyesight and their fast and agile flight as defences against the mountain predators.

Down in the strath the air was still and humid again, stifling and enervating as I walked the last stretch towards the car. The track down to the road wanders through the wooded policies of the old mansion house, once the domain of a team of gardeners and woodmen but now a neglected tangle of shrubs and weeds run wild under a sparse canopy of old Scots pines, semi-exotic trees, and the inevitable scattering of those monkey-puzzle trees that the Victorians loved. These north-western Highland areas are warmed in winter by the last vestiges of the Gulf Stream, suffering few frosts at sea level, and enjoying some of the longest growing seasons of any part of Britain. This douce climate had conspired with a pocket of unusual fertility to produce a wilderness of extraordinarily rich shrub and plant growth. Somewhere within all this tangled growth there flows the lowest stretches of the small stream that rose high in the hills behind, where sea-trout come nosing in on the summer tides between rocky banks that had once been tended and manicured into a succession of arbours and ornamental bowers. It is still just possible to thread your way along the course of the little stream and see the

overgrown remains of the intricate ornamental gardening and landscaping features that had once made the estate famous, in the days of cheap labour before successive death duties had crippled the family's fortunes.

In spring the place is alive with birdsong, but by late July the silence of high summer has fallen on the old gardens. The only sounds I heard as I picked my way down to the stream were the abrupt barking of a startled roe deer that crashed off unseen with a swishing of vegetation, and the distant call of a magpie, a dry rattling call like someone shaking a large and resonant box of matches. A common enough sound in most of the British Isles, where magpies are now far too numerous for those who like their hedgerows to be full of songbirds' nests in spring, the magpie is something of an exotic rarity in the north-west Highlands. Branches and roots of rhododendrons and azaleas did their best to ensnare and trip me as I pushed awkwardly down towards the overgrown shell grotto that had been scooped out of the rocky river bank just below the tall south-facing windows of the great house. It is a place of damp shadows and encroaching mosses and ivy, its rocky walls and over-arching roof studded with countless thousands of shells set in grey mortar. Not just the familiar shells of the limpets and cockles, razor-shells and mussels that litter the white sands of the sea loch, but here and there are leopard-spotted cowrie shells, and conches large and small, pink and pearly and coral red, brought back from remote corners of the Empire to this garden in the Highlands by generations of the lairds' family long dead and buried.

Above the hum of insects and the buzz of gnats and midges in the muggy air I could still hear the magpies' chattering rattle, and I pushed my way out of the tangled shrubbery and back towards the car in the direction of their steady cacophony. Through an unexpected tunnel in the undergrowth I eventually got a good look at them, a party of squat and comically reptilian young, well-feathered in sharp monochrome but with the scruffy and gauche appearance of all young birds, and squawking eager imprecations and beseechings to one of the adults that perched nearby, with filtered sunlight striking an iridescent sheen off that elongated, upward-angled tail that never fails to remind me of the handle of a frying-pan.

Sleep usually comes easily to me, most of all after a long day's tramping on the hill, but by midnight the air was still oppressively muggy, and I lay awake with the bedroom window and door both wide open in a vain attempt to create some cooling draught. Then, just as I felt I was at last dropping off, there came a sound that is one of the best recipes for a sleepless night, the insistent calling of a corncrake in the velvet darkness. It began like the distant sound of a football rattle being whirled, and then as I listened more carefully it settled down to a steady dry

scratching and *crekk*-ing, apparently coming from the hay meadows that lay between the house and the shore of the sea loch.

There was a time when the calling of corncrakes in the night in summer was one of the commonest sounds of rural Britain and Ireland, as familiar by night as the evocative crooning of woodpigeons from the trees by day. Their interminable ratchetings were commonplace in Ireland in my boyhood in the 1950s, and then they suddenly dwindled, becoming fewer each year. In cereal-growing areas of Britain the decline may have been accelerated by the trend towards pesticide spraying and a reduction in the numbers of insects in the standing crops; but in Ireland, which is primarily a livestock grazing country, and over most of the rest of the British Isles the critical factor had been the increasing mechanisation of farming, and especially the trend towards late spring silage cutting instead of traditional summer haymaking. Fast moving machinery can simply be too quick for corncrakes to escape, and the cutting of silage grass from May onwards is far too early for the late-nesting corncrake, and both sitting hens and their eggs and broods were destroyed by the whirling blades of forage harvesters on fields where earlier generations of farmers had waited until July or August to save their crops of hay.

By the 1970s the corncrake decline was so serious and widespread that the most likely places to hear the birds calling were the little crofting fields of the Hebrides and the west Highlands, and in those parts of western Ireland where a few farmers still left their grass to make late hay. One of the most surprising places I ever heard a corncrake was on an area of neglected rough grasses and marshland known as the Bog Meadows, less than a mile from the city centre of Belfast. There, up to the late 1970s, the corncrake was an annual visitor, and there were resident snipe and teal and moorhens too. This had been a traditional rough-shooter's haunt for snipe and duck, and golden plover too, until it became unwise — and highly unpopular with the army and police patrols — to potter about with a shotgun within a few hundred yards of the Falls Road and the strife-torn streets of west Belfast. One of my last visits there in the 1970s was to see a falconer's trained buzzard flown in pursuit of moorhens, over a network of boggy drains and pools that has long since vanished under a wilderness of new factories and industrial estates.

The corncrake's repetitive scratchings and *crekk*-ings can be maddening to anyone trying to get a night's sleep in summer, but even more frustrating are most attempts to find the birds and catch a glimpse of them. They are furtive and skulking creatures, whose plumage is not unlike that of a grey partridge, and they have an uncanny ability to conceal themselves in long grass and standing crops. Almost all the corncrakes I have seen have been no more than quick glimpses of birds scuttling across country roads at the approach of the car, to be lost again in the lush roadside grasses or a field of barley. A dog is a better finder than a man on his own, and may even succeed in springing the bird into flight, which is characterised by a weak wingbeat and heavily trailing legs, so feeble that it seems incredible that they should be capable of making the long migration from sub-Saharan Africa. But beware of using a too-exuberant gundog to locate a corncrake: I remember one rampant spaniel that became quite adept at grabbing the birds as they laboured into flight and retrieving them to its owner!

John Clare, the Northamptonshire poet, described his vain attempts to find a corncrake — 'I have followed it for hours and all to no purpose. It seem'd like a spirit that mock'd my folly in running after it . . . ' — and there is something deceptive and maddeningly elusive about the bird's ventriloquial call, that seems to be coming from one spot and suddenly from somewhere else, presumably an effect caused by the bird turning its head as it calls. I remember how one former politician in Ireland used to be nicknamed 'the corncrake' because of his habit of making incessant speeches and yet always shifting his opinions. 'Yon bloody man's like a corncrake. He never shuts up, but you can never rightly tell which field he's in!'

Now, in the warmth of a west Highland night, I was glad to hear this corncrake's calling, even though his *crekk*-ing monotony robbed me of sleep until long after midnight. He seemed to circle the house, which had grassy meadows and little fields of oats on all sides, calling as he moved about, and he and his family were probably secure from harm since haymaking was still a couple of weeks away, and the oats would not be harvested until September. I eventually drifted off into sleep, and overslept by a couple of hours the next morning.

A few days later I braved the long drive south, past endless caravans and queues of holiday traffic on the A9 and the pelting rush of heavy vehicles on the motorways, and found myself back in Wessex, in the heart of the countryside between Salisbury and Dorchester that is celebrated as the setting for so many of Thomas Hardy's powerful but moodily miserable novels. The fields of wheat and barley that had stood hip-high and golden a few weeks before had now been harvested, leaving wide swathes of close-cropped stubbles. Some had been undersown with fodder turnips, others had already gone under the plough, and the whole landscape had a sudden bareness and openness that already seemed to hint at the coming of autumn. At dawn and again towards dusk I was out and about on a favourite area of wooded farmland, attempting an estimate of the roe deer population. Once the cereal crops get up in spring the deer vanish, and all we can hope for is the occasional glimpse of ears or antler tips above the heads of the corn, or a fleeting sight of deer crossing the narrow bare headlands between the woodland edge and the standing corn as they move to and fro between resting and feeding.

But when the cereals have been harvested, the deer seem to take a little while to realise that they are suddenly no longer invisible. They wander freely about the freshly-shorn fields, with little apparent awareness of just how conspicuous they are, as though they imagined themselves still to be safely veiled from human view. So it is an excellent time to sit with a pair of binoculars and watch them and count them, usually in small family parties with the buck often grazing or resting at a little distance from the doe and her invariable twin kids.

It was a warm and overcast evening, balmy but with no hint of the thundery humidity that had afflicted so much of Britain during the previous ten days. The deer emerged early from their lying-up places in the woods and along the hedgerows, and I had completed my rounds well before nine o'clock, earlier than I had expected. With time in hand, I drove the few miles westwards that brought me to the fringes of a favourite area of Dorset heathland, to revisit a spot where I had found nightjars nesting in previous years, and where I had been lucky enough to see one of the birds earlier that same spring.

A retired forester friend was the self-appointed, unpaid warden of this little wild place, with an intimate knowledge of its creatures and plants and insects that stemmed from long hours and months and years spent there at all sorts of unsocial hours of the day and night. The deer that lived there had him to thank for warning off the louts that used to come from Southampton with ugly lurchers, ready to course and pull down any deer, with equal disregard for the law, the sporting seasons and the cruelty of destroying does heavy in young or with unweaned fawns. The thoughtless picnicers who abandoned their litter there were quite unaware that the pristine loveliness of the place was only maintained by this dedicated man, who regularly cleared up after them and filled several bags with their trash every week, carrying it off in the back of his little van to be dumped on the council tip.

We had met there on the heath early on a May morning, to watch for deer and look for early wild orchids, when his eye had fallen unerringly on a nightjar roosting motionless on the ground. He was stretched out in contented stillness on a bed of leaf litter just a few feet to one side of the little path, clearly an adult male with those tell-tale pale tips to his outer tail feathers. Against the dead leaves he was perfectly camouflaged, his mottled plumage of duns and russets and subtle greys breaking up his outline and blending with all around him. From a distance of less than twenty feet we stood quietly and focussed

our binoculars on him, able to study each tiny detail as he lay as still and sombre as a piece of fallen branch.

Around his chosen resting place there rose the fresh greenery of the new season's growth of bracken, succulent pale shoots that jutted up with their unfolding heads curled over and folded back like the intricate carving on a bishop's pastoral staff, or the elaborately-wrought handle of an ornate shepherd's crook. What an irony that this pernicious and invasive weed, so threatening to many habitats by its steady expansion in much of Britain, looks so attractive at this early stage of growth. In the magnified circle of the binoculars' field of view we could see the downward slant of the nightjar's mandibles, that mouth that could gape so wide when the bird was hunting, and distinguish the delicate whiskery filaments that fringed both sides of its head, sensitive antennae for locating insects on the wing in the darkest nights.

He is a gawky, almost ugly bird, with all the primitive gaucherie that can also be seen in his cousin the cuckoo; an ancient species whose appearance at rest hints at the reptile origins of birds, and whose flight has much of the same hawk-like movement that causes so many small birds to mob the day-flying cuckoo. Here in Wessex they call him the fern hawk or the fern owl, and elsewhere in Britain he is known as the gnat hawk and the moth hawk, the latter names incorporating allusion both to his hawking manner of flight and to his habit of feeding on insects by night. The official manuals tell us his formal name is *Caprimulgus europaeus* — literally, the 'European goat-milker' — and this is reflected in another widespread country name in southern and eastern England, the goat-sucker. Ancient beliefs, in Britain and across the Mediterranean, and stretching back into classical Greece, held that the nightjar sucked the milk of goats and sheep and cattle from their udders by night, and not only was this nocturnal theft a mysterious and ominous activity in itself, it was also invested with an added dimension of avian vampirism because it was thought that the suckling bird poisoned the beasts it milked. In parts of England this infection was known as 'the puck' and from it stems another south of England name for the bird, the puckeridge. And Puck, the impish spirit of English folklore, also has his associations with milk, having allegedly been able to weave a mischievous charm that deprived milk of its cream and made it impossible for it to be churned into butter, cheese and whey.

We left our fern owl still roosting quietly and appropriately among the emerging fronds of fern, and moved carefully away to avoid frightening him off. It could not have been very long since he had made his return flight from his wintering grounds in Africa, and we were eager that no disturbance should drive him away and prevent another breeding success this year.

That first sighting of the year had been about twelve weeks earlier, and by now, with luck, that male and his mate should be well established and nesting somewhere on the heath. At least it was worth a wait, to see if I could locate them or hear the birds singing as dusk gathered. The conditions made me optimistic, since nightjars tend to display and sing best on warm, still evenings like this, when the multitude of insects provides them with plentiful feeding. So I sat down quietly at the base of a small birch that grew alongside one of the main rides through the heath, from where I had a good view westwards, so that any birds that appeared on the wing would be silhouetted against the last of the light in the sky.

A woodcock was first to appear, and perhaps more that one woodcock, as I saw a succession of individual fleeting shapes skimming above the low clumps of gorse and among the scattered birches, some silent and perhaps simply flighting off to feed, while one or two other passing birds made the distinctive croak-and-*twisick* calls that are so instantly indicative of male woodcock roding. The latter sightings, four in all, were almost certainly the same bird seen four times, beating the bounds of his displaying territory as the light began to dim, in hopes of attracting the answering signals of a female ready to mate.

A fox, quite unaware of me hunched and motionless at the base of the tree, emerged from cover about forty yards ahead, paused briefly, and then trotted along the sandy path towards me for a few yards, before something seemed to catch his attention, and made him stop again; and then he made a sharp move off at a tangent, his nose held a little higher as if he was suddenly on the scent of something new and interesting.

The light had drained out of the landscape to the stage where everything had assumed a uniform hue of greyish-brown when I had my first glimpse of a nightjar, a long-tailed, lop-winged shape that flew low and uncertainly across the heath, then banked and gained height towards a small stand of Scots pines, and was lost to sight against their darkness. Another five or six minutes passed, and then I heard a sound as though some piece of machinery had suddenly been switched on. It began abruptly, a sustained sound of soft and resonant whirring, like a fast but muted ratchet, but not muffled, and gradually pervading the soft stillness of the twilight as if I was sitting inside some throbbing chamber like a ship's hold. It was difficult to identify its source, first seeming to come from the general direction of the distant pines off to my left, then appearing to come from behind me, then from somewhere out in front — the steady and insistently gentle *churr*-ing of a nightjar, unlike any other sound in the countryside. It *churr*-ed, then paused, then *churr*-ed again for almost an hour, by which time a combination of cramp and sleepiness made me pull myself to my feet, the tingling of pins-and-needles in my legs ebbing away as I made my way back to the car as quietly as I could.

Along the Woodland Edge

There are few things as dead as a midsummer's day. Everything in the natural world seems to have gone to sleep, or to be held in some form of suspended animation. The leaves hang heavy on the trees, dark green and leaden compared with the fresh animation of spring growth. The birds have stopped singing their spring songs of territorial aggression and breeding contact. The river is low and sluggish, its water looking like syrup or honey in the pools between the bleached stones with their crusted caps of dried-out weed and mosses. The rookery is almost abandoned, its ceaseless springtime clamour ended for another year, and only an occasional bird flopping listlessly among the upper branches of the trees, mostly hidden by the thick foliage. The fields are rank with long grasses, docks and thistles. And the best times to see and hear wild creatures are in the cool and dewy hours at dawn and dusk, before the sun has got up high, and again after it has drooped and allowed long shadows to invade the landscape as darkness falls.

But dogs still have to be walked, the river has to be checked for poachers, and legs must be stretched, even when the sun is high and we're likely to see very little of interest. Below the bridge a dipper comes zipping down the stream, stops and perches hesitantly on a stone, its bill stuffed with what looks like a transverse wedge of dry grasses, but is in fact a straggly bundle of insects. It bobs and curtseys briefly and then is off again, skimming just above the low pools and swinging up to land by its nest under the old stone parapet, where a late brood is on the point of fledging. Dippers seem to be especially fond of nesting on man-made structures such as bridges and piers and weirs, perhaps because they offer nesting niches that are particularly well hidden out of sight of potential avian predators, and more secure from mink and stoats and weasels than if they were to make use of one of the innumerable nooks in the natural riverside rocks and rocky slabs. I have even found one pair of dippers nesting right inside the rusting remains of an old car that had been shoved into a river, not an asset to the pastoral ambience of what was otherwise a very pretty stretch of river, but presumably as safe a place as any in which to lay your eggs and rear your young.

High overhead a buzzard is swinging in lazy widening circles on the thermals, seemingly too relaxed even to give its customary mewing calls. In the larches a woodpigeon, content to call but not energetic enough to fly, coos its soft repetitive *continuo* that is distantly answered by another from the line of old beeches far down the valley.

The local rabbits, though active mainly in the cool of dusk and dawn, occasionally lie out by day, basking in the warmth of a sunny tussock of grass or on a warm bank of exposed earth. Their distribution hereabouts is something of a puzzle, and in almost six years we have had only two of them on our few acres on the south side of the river, while the northern bank abounds with them. Those two vagrants gave our dogs unlimited mileage in the form of incessant chasings without ever being caught, from which we concluded that either our dogs are very inept, which is unlikely in view of their general standard of performance on bunnies elsewhere, or that these rabbits had unusually charmed lives and had been sent by Providence to give our deprived dogs some fun on their own doorstep. In any event, we decided that both must have been males, since no young ones materialised; and they remain very scarce in our immediate vicinity.

The river is certainly no barrier to them, at least in summer when its levels are so low, sometimes for weeks on end, that even a fieldmouse might skip across dry-shod. On our side the reddish earth, the crumbling shales and the well-drained slopes would make just as good burrowing ground for them as any on the northern side. But still they do not come, for some reason probably known only to rabbits. Perhaps this is a bonus for the garden; but we still think it's a pity that the dogs, devoted rabbit chasers all, are deprived of the fun of the hunt on their home ground, and have to make do with the occasional opportunity that arises when we venture further afield with them across the little river valley.

To the north of the river the land rises very gradually, a scattering of lush pastures interspersed with random blocks and strips of conifers, and a few older copses of mixed oak and ash. At some stage many of the fields have been enlarged, the old hedgerows with their standards of ash and beech cut away to leave straight raised ridges of grass over light soil where the main colonies of rabbits occur.

One evening I went there a couple of hours before dusk in late June, not with a pack of dogs this time, as I was watching for roe deer, and had taken only my old labrador, which I left at a distance in the car. I worked my way along the edge of a spruce belt on the shadowy eastern side, where deer sometimes emerge, and chose a place to sit down on a small hummock, my back against the plantation fence. I sat and watched and waited and smoked a cigar, not just as a sybaritic indulgence, but because smoke is the subtlest of all wind indicators. I watched the threads of drifting blue-grey smoke for confirmation of the direction of the light breeze. A jay screamed intermittently back in the trees behind me, and a carrion crow flapped steadily off across the open field towards the blue-green line of spruces in the distance.

The ability to stand (or even sit) quite still, alone and silent, is a rare accomplishment in contemporary man. Modern life is so taken up with movement, noise and activity that the passive, silent and watchful mode is increasingly hard to adopt. Those of us who spend our typical working days in the bustle of traffic, at crowded meetings, among the incessant electronic activity of an office desk, stimulated and interrupted by phones and faxes and computer screens, are likely to find it militates against the capacity to move carefully, to watch and wait and listen and be still. To see and study most wild creatures and their ways, our insistent, compulsive activity has to be replaced by alert passivity, and the change is not an easy one to make. He who marches briskly about the woods and fields may get good healthy exercise, but he will not see or hear half as much as he who simply chooses a likely spot and.just keeps still, and waits, and watches. And it is no easy option, this silent vigilance: anyone who manages to spend a couple of hours motionless, fully alert and watchful in the countryside will find it is exhausting in its own way. To feel drained and tired by long stillness and watching and listening is inevitable, and much of the stress stems from the very unfamiliarity of behaving like this, rather like the aches that come from using unfamiliar muscles. Anyone who disbelieves this should try accompanying an experienced woodland deer stalker for a couple of hours at dawn and dusk, and will quickly learn that there is a special strain in keeping all your senses keen and poised while you take fully half an hour to move barely a hundred yards. 'Study to be quiet', counselled Izaak Walton in 1653; and it is not an easy skill to master. Running a marathon may seem the easier option by comparison.

To my right and marking the corner of the plantation was a mature trio of larches and an old Scots pine, and as I turned my head that way a slight movement caught my eye. The binoculars revealed a tree creeper, questing in the crevices of the bark for insects. Its progress was thoughtful and methodical, involving longish pauses while it balanced with legs outspread and feet gripping the crinkled skin of the bark, the depressed chestnut feathers of its tail providing it with a firm prop from below, rather as one might perch on a shooting stick. Its neat head with the pale eye-stripe and the delicately down-curved and pointed spike of the bill gave it an appearance of precise, almost surgically meticulous concentration, and as it moved sideways on to me I could clearly see the almost silvery whiteness of its throat, breast and belly feathers, a superb natural adaptation to reflect the maximum amount of available light into the interstices and wrinkles of the rough bark and expose the presence of insects and other food lurking there. I watched intermittently as it moved up each of the four trees' trunks in turn, submitting each to a slow and rigorous search, and demonstrating as it did so how superb was its balance and grip, often not needing to make use of its tail as a prop, and evidently maintaining an excellent hold with those outspread feet. It even managed to impart a considerable air of poise and grace to an activity that was in many ways undignified, its postures often oddly froglike and squatting.

Eventually I felt the wire strand of the fence twitch momentarily against my back, and heard it twang and grate slightly against the rusty staples that secured it. A deer pushing out, perhaps? But there were no signs. Then, from slightly uphill to my left, came a high squeal. Not a roe kid, by the sound of it; more like a rabbit. I twisted round slowly and raised the binoculars to look up the side of the plantation. About fifty yards up the woodland edge there was a huddled shape, dun coloured and motionless. Then it moved abruptly, flicking up its head and ears to show it was indeed a rabbit. Another thin, attenuated squeal came down the breeze, and the rabbit again huddled down in a hunched position. There was a quick flash of vivid foxy-red against the green of the grass and contrasting with the dull brown of the young rabbit's coat, and a stoat bounced up from the tussocky grass. In the binoculars I could clearly see its bright button eyes, its rounded alert ears, the creamy white of its undercoat, and the sable tip of its tail that twitched erect.

Still the rabbit was motionless, hunched in the tussocky grass, and the stoat flicked sideways and seemed to slip away through the mesh of the fence. Then it was back again in a bounding, undulating run, springing over the longer grasses and landing four-square on the rabbit's back again, pausing and seeming to writhe and squirm, then off again as another squealing cry came from the hump of dun fur that lolloped forwards a couple of feet, its head low and ears flattened back, and squatted again.

The stylised sophistication in a stoat's deadly play with a rabbit is something every observant country dweller will see sooner or later, though perhaps less often now than in the pre-myxomatosis days of 1953–54, when rabbits filled the fields and hedgerows in their millions. It has all the slow terror, taunting and wilfully protracted, of a cat's encounter with a mouse; but there is something extra, too, an added dimension of slick and sinuous refinement that makes it seem the quintessence of exquisite cruelty. The huddled bundle of trembling fur in the grass seems both pathetic and phlegmatic compared with the lithe agility of its tormentor, whose flashing vitality encircles the rabbit in a web of inescapable horror. More than almost any other encounter of predator with prey to be seen in Britain, it invites all the immediate anthropomorphic repugnance we can feel, this timid ball of fur so evocative of nursery tales of Peter Rabbit and the Flopsy Bunnies, and this sleek and snake-like mustelid that will not kill it cleanly, but instead dances and weaves and bites and holds its half-dead victim in a mesmeric charm woven by its dance of death. There is a grotesque yet horrified fascination when we see it, as if we too were somehow under the stoat's spell, unable to move or intervene to end the hideous drama, until something in us snaps and we reach for a clod of earth or a stone to fling at the pair, driving the attacker off and leaving us to pick up a rabbit paralysed by terror and pain, and probably likely to succumb quickly to pure shock.

We are torn between sentimentality and realism. The stoat's encounter with the rabbit, so often described, yet so perfectly indescribable, is a great antidote to the sentimental temptations of so much nature observation and writing. Here is the bitter redness of Nature's teeth and claws in all its uncompromising harshness. And yet the stoat must live too, and the same drama is enacted daily by a million stoats and a million rabbits.

> Are God and Nature then at strife,
> That Nature lends such evil dreams?
> So careful of the type she seems,
> So heedless of the single life.

The stoat and the rabbit exist in a dynamic natural equilibrium that we can only seek dimly to understand, as Tennyson tried to do. The single life is transitory and expendable, existing perhaps only for the purpose of passing on its genes and maintaining the type, the species. And even the extinction of species seems to play a part in the larger drama of evolution, although the conventional wisdom of the conservation movement is that we must move heaven and earth to save any species from extinction. Yet there are others, anguished by what they see as the exploitation of species, who yearn for extinctions: the death of the last whale will mean an end to all whale suffering. Mankind creates exquisite moral dilemmas for itself.

I sat still and waited. The screams came feebler and less often now. Then the huddle of fur rolled slowly sideways and the greyish-white of its belly fur was visible in the grasses. Then it again jerked and twitched, and moved towards the fence, the body tugged along by the stoat, until it was pulled out of sight into the shadow of the trees. Just ten yards further up the plantation edge two other young rabbits were feeding and playing, quite unaware of the stoat's presence and the fate of its victim.

The warm evening grew more close and muggy, and a thin gauze of midges filled the humid air. Still no sign of deer. Then a high, reedy call came from behind and above me, followed by a soft guttural note. A dark shape flicked out above the tops of the trees, a brown bird that beat along on steady wings, angling in a wide curve across the field and around to the right, to swing back towards the woods. In the binoculars' image it was clear, a bird the size of a pigeon, with wings that were broad and long and pointed, a short and rounded tail, and a thin projecting bill that opened and closed as it flew. *Twis-ick.* The thin, high call came again, its two quick syllables rising in tone and emphasis on the second note, with a deep and croaking note to follow, repeated several times. *Twis-ick* again, and more deep, soft gutturals. A woodcock was on the wing in one of its dusk displays. Ten, twelve, a score of times I counted it passing overhead, flying steadily on the same unvarying, looping course above the wood and the neighbouring pastures, each circuit taking just over two minutes as I listened and watched and timed its repeated movements.

The breeding woodcock of spring and summer are quite different birds from the silent, flickering wraiths of russet brown that are sprung from cover on winter shooting days. The silence and seclusion of their winter ways have been abandoned, for this is the time when the resident breeding males have to adopt an uncharacteristically self-advertising style of display, proclaiming their presence to any receptive females that may be watching and listening. This is the time of the roding.

In France they call it *la croule*, and in much of northern Europe it has always been an important time in the sporting calendar, when the woodcock return to their unfrozen breeding haunts from which they fled south-westwards with the onset of last autumn's frosts. Today, only a few European regions still permit woodcock shooting in spring, understandably reluctant to allow the shooting of a bird that is advertising for a mate.

Contrary to the general trend of wild gamebirds and waterfowl, woodcock numbers in Britain and Ireland are actually on the increase, a pattern that can be traced back for at least fifty years. Winter numbers have probably not been higher in historic times, and much of this can be attributed to the vastly greater acreage of good wintering cover that has been created by the planting of post-war commercial forests. Woodcock like dark, silent, frost-free places with a good covering of evergreen growth, the perfect description of tens of thousands of acres of spruce and pine plantations across northern and western Britain. A few traditionalists doubted the potential of conifers to hold woodcock, for the curious reason that these birds were unlikely to feel comfortable when roosting on a carpet of sharp pine needles! This view failed to take into account that the huge northern forests where woodcock breed in Scandinavia and Russia are composed chiefly of pine trees. Place the bare palm of your hand flat on the carpet of pine needles on the floor of a pine forest and you can feel how soft and well drained it is, ideal for a bird that prefers to roost by day in mild conditions in the quiet seclusion of cover.

Even in times of sharp frost and heavy snow, the conifers keep the woodland floor comparatively warm and dry; there is little or no disturbance from livestock or the busily active pheasants that prefer mixed woodlands; and most of the new forests are never visited by dogs and guns for seasons on end. The Victorian sportsmen knew the west of Ireland and the north of Scotland as largely treeless landscapes, where woodcock would pack in dense numbers into whatever coverts were available when hard weather came along, hence the prodigious bags of 'cock they made at Ashford in Galway, and in the hazel, birch and ash woods along the sides of Loch Ness. A century and more later, these areas are widely afforested with conifers, and they still attract large numbers of woodcock, probably more than ever before, but now spread widely and thinly over much increased acreages of good wintering habitat.

And more and more appear to be staying to join the resident breeding woodcock population. A generation or more ago, the finding of a woodcock's nest was something of an event; now woodcock breed in all suitable woods across the mainlands of the British

Isles, except for Cornwall and the far south-west of Ireland — ironically the places *par excellence* for high densities of woodcock in winter.

To find a woodcock's nest, avoid the woods in daytime. Then the hen bird sits tight on her eggs, the superb cryptic camouflage of her plumage of russets and browns and buffs providing the perfect concealment. She sits motionless, even when man or dog come within a few feet, and your best chance of spotting her is to catch the sheen of her large and lustrous eye, like a shiny bead. At night, too, the hen bird sits tight, but tends to leave her eggs at dawn and dusk, to feed and drink on the woodland floor not far from her nesting place. Uncovered, the eggs seem surprisingly pale and shinily conspicuous in the subdued light under the forest canopy, and you may spot them some way off — as may sharp-eyed predators such as magpies and crows. Otherwise an opportunistic fox or a feral cat is the greatest threat to a nesting woodcock and her eggs, should either happen to come across them.

Do woodcock really carry their young in flight? Of course they do! At any rate, *some* do, on *some* occasions. And yet those who have not seen it with their own eyes can be vigorously, almost angrily opposed to the very suggestion. I have never seen a whale giving birth, or a sea-otter beaking open clams with a rocky hammer, but I wouldn't dream of arguing with the many reliable and honest witnesses who have. The same credence is due to the many trustworthy witnesses who have seen the woodcock airlift. And I'm afraid there would be no point in offering a prize for the first person to come up with a photograph of a woodcock carrying a chick in flight: a captive mother and chick, a dab of superglue on the downy chick, would be all too easy to arrange, and "shure, the world is full of trickery", as an Irish ghillie friend once solemnly remarked to me. A thick volume could be filled with the written accounts of those who have seen woodcock airlifting their young, and the reports are very consistent. Invariably the adult bird — presumably the mother, although woodcock cannot be sexed from external characteristics — is seen to rise heavily and fly off slowly with a leaden, lurching flight, usually with her tail depressed in the shape of a lobster's tail, and with a single chick held between her legs or thighs. And how do we dismiss the testimony of the considerable number of witnesses who have been lucky enough to see a woodcock fly off with one chick, deposit it at a distance, and return to airlift another, and even a third or fourth?

It is not typical or very common for woodcock to carry their young, nor is it especially uncommon. When it does occur, it seems usually to be either in response to the intrusion of a potential threat — perhaps the observer himself — or as a means of moving small chicks to a more suitable place for them to feed.

A thin mist was beginning to gather like fine smoke in the valley bottom as I made my way back to the car. Rounding a hedgerow corner I startled a brown bird that flickered into flight, a fleeting image of deep russets and long wings that I at first thought to be a woodcock, but a second later resolved itself into the distinctive shape of a kestrel, an adult male with ashen-grey head and tail and slate-coloured wingtips. Presumably I had surprised it on some prey, but I could find nothing from a quick search of the grass where it had risen. It made off fast, climbing as it went, and breasted the tops of a belt of mature spruces, curling around and appearing to catch some lift from a breeze or a thermal, although the air seemed quite still and heavy. It set its wings in a high glide, then gave a few shallow wingbeats, and suddenly stopped dead in mid-air, about a hundred yards away from me. Its tail was outspread and slightly depressed, and its wings flickered and shimmered as it hovered, holding itself perfectly on station, its head bowed and looking fixedly downwards.

I steadied myself against the corner straining post of the fence and brought the stalking telescope to bear on the motionless kestrel, its every detail suddenly clear and vivid in the eyepiece. Sideways on to me, its head was visible in perfect profile, the waxen yellow of its cere and the lustrous velvet brown of its eye quite bright and clear against the grey of the sky. Every little tremor of those fluttering wings and that dipping tail was dedicated to keeping the bird's head absolutely still, the natural equivalent of a gyroscopic stabiliser, so that it could minutely scan the pasture that lay about sixty feet below. It checked, lost a few feet of height, then steadied again, lowering first one golden yellow foot and then the other as if it were stretching or limbering up for a dive and grab. Then it was off, its wings set in a curling glide that took it around the far end of the spruces and out of sight beyond a clump of hazel bushes and into the valley below.

Back at the car the old labrador rose and yawned and stretched and thumped her tail. Then, realising that I had brought nothing new back with me, she yawned again, rolled her eyes in lugubrious boredom, and curled up with a deep grumble of sleepy contentment. It was time for us both to go home.

Encounters by
the Hidden Loch

Far in the west there is a long ridge of heathery hills, that hunches up against the sky like the low hull of a submarine. The ordnance survey map shows that the broad plateau along its back is spangled with little lochs, like a scattering of sapphire chips on a background of terracotta browns. Some are barely more than large puddles in the blanket peat, yet each has its own Gaelic name, evocative to read and melodious to hear on the lips of the local people. 'There's plenty of trout in them', we were told, 'and some good big ones, too, if you can catch them, in Loch . . . .' And our local expert uttered a soft Gaelic name. I was sworn to secrecy then, and I will keep the name a secret still, for what we found there would be in peril if it was to become too widely known.

The map helped us to plan our approach for the next day. We would drive to the end of the peat-cutters' track and park there, before going the final two miles over the heather and the rough deer grass on foot. Allow two hours or so for walking there and back, make an early start, and we should have a good long day for exploring. The weather forecast was good, promising a mild day of high cloud and intermittent late July sunshine — good weather for the hills, if we charitably assumed they had got their prediction right for this remote region of glens and moors, which isn't always the case.

It was just after nine o'clock when we locked the car, more from habit than necessity in this lonely spot, and struck off up the hill. An Irish setter, a glowing mahogany streak of lean energy, quartered ahead of us, racing to and fro across the gentle southerly breeze, revelling in its inbred urge to quest for the air scent of game. This is grouse country, not the manicured moorland of northern England or the Scottish Borders, but a wild expanse of heather and bilberry cropped by a few semi-wild blackface sheep. There are grouse here, but you need strong legs and good lungs to follow a questing setter in search of the scattered coveys. Meantime our thoughts were on the hill birds, the lochs, and their fish. We each wore a small haversack with waterproofs and some food, and from both there protruded a short tubular case holding a multi-sectioned fishing rod. A handful of small collecting bottles clinked gently in the pockets of our bags as we tramped, for bringing back any specimens we might decide to take for further study.

There was a wild and fluting call of golden plover on the breeze as we picked our way carefully up through the long heather, the soggy sphagnum pools and the tumbled granite boulders. A greenish-purple sheen clung to our boots and a fine haze of dust swirled in the air as our footsteps kicked up puffs of heather pollen. Sunlight and a light wind kept the midges away, but the air was full of tiny gnats and the heather flies of late summer, flying slowly and seeming almost to hover with dangling legs, like little parachutists. The sphagnum pools were fringed with rank rushes, which swarmed with craneflies. No shortage of daddy-longlegs here for whatever grouse chicks had hatched and managed to escape the attentions of harriers and foxes. We were making good headway, legs and lungs becoming attuned as we got our second wind.

A couple of hundred yards ahead and off to our left, the setter suddenly slowed to a brisk, stiff-legged walk and spun into the wind, then halted in a half crouch with her feathered tail held outstretched and low. In unison we quickened our pace as much as the gradient would allow, and converged on the unmoving dog. She rolled her eyes sideways to see if we were coming, and her lips were curled upwards to make the most of the current of scent that was flowing down the breeze and into her nose. Close behind her now, a click of my fingers made her rise slightly from her crouching set and inch forwards, her head low and her tail lashing gently from side to side. Then she dropped on her belly as the heather just yards in front of her was suddenly alive with a flurry of small brown shapes and two much larger ones, a pair of grouse and their late brood of tiny cheepers. The dark-coloured cock swung up and away on the breeze, cackling his *kok-kok-ko-kok-ge'bak-ge'bak-ge'bak* of indignant alarm over his shoulder as he sped away. The hen bird skimmed off forwards and dipped silently out of sight, while the chicks flew in a blur of tiny wings and then landed with awkward, collapsing movements one by one into the longer cover ahead, cheeping and calling among the rank stalks of old heather. A very late brood, and perhaps a second attempt after a fox or a hooded crow had destroyed the first eggs or young; and we turned and led the setter away to allow the birds to regroup and reunite as they responded to each other's contact calls.

Beyond the crest of the ridge the ground levelled out and we moved into a chaos of dark peat hags, a landscape of miniature plains of black peaty mud overhung by abrupt little cliffs of heather, where it was impossible for us to walk a straight course. We scrambled onto the top of one of the higher tussocky knolls and looked around. There in the distance, glimpsed in a low fold of the plateau, was a glint of water, its surface reflecting the blue of a now cloudless sky to the south. The *koo-eee* flutings of plover were louder and nearer now, and a flicker of wings showed where a small flock was just pitching down on the fringe of a bare patch of hill where a shepherd's match had fired the old heather in spring.

I pulled my stalking glass from my knapsack and extended the tubes, squinting and twisting the eyepiece to find a clear focus, and then the fuzzy image leapt into sudden crispness, the magnified picture shimmering slightly in the warm air. The plover were standing among a low forest of blackened heather stalks, bodies and heads erect, rounded breasts swelled out, and with the pale band over the eye and curving down the side of the head clearly visible. A few stood motionless, heads into the wind, while others stretched their wings, first one side and then the other, revealing a pale flash of feathering on the underside of their pinions. Some scuttled and stopped, scuttled and stopped repeatedly among the burnt heather, and one lay down and stretched itself with wings outspread to bask on the sun-warmed surface of the exposed peat. Soon, perhaps in another month or so, these plover families would begin moving down to the lower meadows and the fields along the coast which would be their autumn and winter quarters, where they would shortly be joined by wheeling, piping flocks of migrant cousins who had come south from Scandinavia and Iceland for the winter.

The intimate circular image of the telescope allowed me to examine the birds almost one by one, quite unaware that they were being watched. A glint of something bright made me stare long and hard at one bird before I eventually got a clear view of its legs and saw that it was wearing a metal leg-band. Then another of the group scuttled out from among tufty heather shoots and stood still on the bare peat, revealing that it too had been ringed. Nestlings that had been ringed in late spring by the local doctor? I knew he was a keen and expert ringer, and made a mental note to ask him. Or perhaps these were adults, that had been caught and ringed on their wintering grounds last season or earlier. Then, as suddenly as they had alighted, the little flock leapt into flight again, calling to one another in a clear melodious counterpoint as they flew off with shallow, flickering wingbeats.

The little loch beckoned us, and I took a long look at it with the telescope. It seemed narrow, with a fringe of spiky reeds, and there were two ducks of some kind on the water, teal perhaps, but too far off to be certain. Here on the plateau the ground was waterlogged, despite a dry spell for several weeks before, and we squelched and sploshed along, threading a careful way through treacherous networks of sphagnum pools, each with its floating mantle of yellowish-green that overlay who knows what fathomless depths of liquid peat: not a place to cross in thick mist or at night. Local legends abound with tales of shepherds who vanished in these hills, of farmers' sons who went over the moors to court girls in distant glens, never to return, their bodies lost in the primeval ooze of bog-holes. Undaunted, the setter raced about, raising a spray of water droplets in her wake, and floundering in and out of the boggy pools with zestful indifference. Dogs are indifferent to cautionary tales. Twice she stopped and froze, marking the presence of squatting snipe, that rose reluctantly and flew feebly when she roaded in to work out her point. These were post-breeding adult snipe, now deep in the late summer moult, and pale ghosts of the plump, dashing fliers we would find on the lower marshes in winter.

Then she stopped and set firmly once again, downwind of a mound of tussocky deer grass, but this time her ears were cocked and her head tilted at an odd angle. Her tail feathered to and fro gently, in contrast to its usual low-set stiffness. Something she was uncertain of? Or perhaps she was feeling a little bit guilty at setting something I expect her to ignore — a hare, perhaps, or maybe even a pipit or a skylark, though she did not seem tired enough to be larking about. Then all at once the air in front of her was filled with the rising, floating shape of a large pale bird with soft, broad wings. A short-eared owl had been resting there in the long grass, perhaps devouring or digesting some recent prey, although we couldn't find any remains after a thorough search of the little knoll. But we did eventually come upon one large, firm pellet of fine fur, hair and little bones where she had regurgitated the fibrous roughage of her last meal, the indigestible residues that remain compacted in the bird's crop, which falconers since ancient times have known are so important for the health of birds of prey.

It was time to slip the lead onto the setter. Whatever those birds were that I had spotted on the loch would be sure to take fright at the bounding appearance of a dog, and probably before we had got close enough to have a good look at them. Unusually for a setter, this one was not a puller; once she felt the slip-lead around her neck she fell submissively to heel, perhaps glad of a rest after those endless quarterings. We were in a slight dip now, with the loch a couple of hundred yards ahead and just out of sight over the next crest. We walked the last stretch quietly, and peered cautiously over the final heathery ridge to the water forty yards beyond and below.

A small party of teal were resting on the water. The light but steady breeze made a ripple of wavelets, and the ducks bobbed gently not far out from the opposite bank. Two were asleep, heads tucked backwards, while others splashed and dabbled close in towards the overhanging bank of peat with its top-knot of tufted heather. I looped the dog's lead over one of my boots to secure her, and she lay and heaved and panted in the long grasses behind me while I flattened myself on a springy bed of long heather and brought the telescope to bear on the teal.

From there I swept the glass over the loch for other signs of life. Another teal, making eight in all, bobbed at rest a little way apart from the others, but that seemed to be all there was. Then I caught a hint of movement at the far end of the loch, where it narrowed towards the eastern end. Nothing distinct as yet, and I twisted the eyepiece gently in search of a crisper focus. No, perhaps I had been mistaken — but wait, there was another movement and now I had a clear view of a small  waterbird of some sort, just besides the tuft of greenish reeds at the extreme end of the loch. It wasn't swimming like a teal, or wading like a snipe — and it wasn't alone, for another one suddenly appeared in the narrow field of the telescope's view. A mystery; these two little birds that moved about steadily in a small area of water close to the far shore, so close that they were not clearly silhouetted against the water, and it was difficult at this distance to make out any details of colour or plumage. What could they be?

We held a brief council of war and decided on a roundabout approach, moving back down into the dead ground below the loch and then round to our right, moving towards the eastern end of the loch but keeping out of sight as we walked. When we judged we were level with the end of the loch, we struck up the gentle slope to the right and crept carefully to look over the crest. There below us and not more than thirty yards away was a shallow delta of rushes where the loch came to a point, beyond which there stretched a soggy-looking area of tufty cotton-grass interspersed with vivid green sphagnum flushes and more reeds. And there were the birds, not two this time but three.

They were phalaropes. There was no mistaking the elfin delicacy of their trim bodies, with necks upstretched and the dark little spikes of their bills jutting almost horizontally. And, the surest sign of all, there was a broad and emphatic dark eye stripe that curved backwards and slightly downwards across the pale sides of the birds' heads — the phalarope-stripe that distinguishes these little wading birds from others. I had seen phalaropes before, the famous red-necked phalaropes that had nested in well-guarded secrecy on a lough in the far west of Ireland, but those I had seen there were adult breeding birds in May, in quite different plumage from these. These three were an exciting find, and they were undoubtedly phalaropes, but we were still puzzled by their appearance.

These were dark-coloured birds, a deep brown on their backs and upper parts, with hints of lighter feather markings that reminded us of snipe, but their throats and upper breasts were pale, and there was no hint of the reddish collar I had seen on those breeding birds in Ireland. We discussed the birds in barely a whisper, we peered endlessly through binoculars and telescope, we sketched in pencil on some sheets of paper — and then light began to dawn. Perhaps — no, certainly — these were young birds. It seemed incredible — three youngsters, probably siblings, of one of the rarest breeding birds in Britain! Dozens of questions raced through our minds. Had they bred here, on this little loch? Might the adults be here somewhere too? Or could they have nested elsewhere? Could these young just be stopping over here? The nearest recent phalarope nesting sites we knew of were in the Western Isles, not here on the mainland. But, after all, the isles were not so very far away.

Questions, endless exciting questions, gave way to watching. We lay in the sun-warmed heather and peered down on the birds, which continued to move about in that same shallow corner of the loch where we had first spotted them, and quite unaware that they were being minutely studied. Small, as small as jack snipe, they pottered about silently and quite contentedly, preening and resting and feeding in a desultory way. They did not wade and feed like snipe, probing in shallow water for food in the mud and peat. Instead they floated in barely a few inches of water, and spun and twirled about, this way and that, first clockwise, then anti-clockwise, and pecked delicately yet briskly at the surface of the water, picking up tiny morsels of food that their twirlings and paddlings had churned up from the shallow peaty mud just below the surface. Each seemed to have singled out a feeding area of about two or three square yards of shallow water as its own, just a little apart from the others, and they busied themselves there for ages. Despite the much more muted coloration of these birds, they brought back increasingly vivid memories of watching those nesting adult phalaropes in May and June in years gone by.

A scrap of birdie doggerel tucked away in my memory crept into my mind:

The phalarope, although red-necked,
Is also dreadfully hen-pecked . . .

(I haven't the least idea who wrote this, or where I first read or heard it, so I can't give the author credit.) No 'red-neck' in the human sense, the poor male phalarope in breeding plumage is denied the usual avian privilege of being brighter and more exotic in looks than his mate. Instead it is she who catches the eye in spring, with that bright sweep of reddish-mahogany on her neck, that curves up like an inverted question-mark behind her eyes, while the male's markings are smaller and a more muted pastel shade.

Already it had been quite a day, but still we had not reached our primary objective, the little loch where the trout of our dreams were said to swim, and so we dragged ourselves away, anticipation mingled with regret at leaving the phalaropes. By just before two o'clock we were in sight of our ultimate goal, the little loch with the soft Gaelic name. Our first glimpse was of a shimmer of glittering blue directly up-sun, then suddenly clearer and less dazzling as another galleon of heaped-up high cumulus cloud sailed across the sun and softened the light. Its few acres, perhaps eight or nine in all, lay cupped in a gentle hollow of the hills, with a fringe of reeds around the southern shore and a scattering of what looked like tiny sandy beaches along its margins.

Ten minutes of steady walking through the last of the heather and grasses had us standing on the first of those little bays, where the heather gave way to a scattering of granite rocks whose tiny facets of mica-schist glinted in the bright light, and then a yard or two of silvery sand against which tiny wavelets a hand's-breadth high lapped gently. This little tarn was different from the others; no peat-gloomy waters beneath low escarpments of undercut turf and heather, but a bright clarity overlying pale sand and marls, and a profusion of insects and small water creatures. The pressure of a booted foot in the shallows made the sand bulge and bubble upwards, like the bursting of a boil or the plopping glug of hot mud in a volcanic spring, and the few inches of pellucid water went suddenly cloudy with a creamy silt. A scooped handful looked like pure kaolin, china clay that promised an alkaline richness quite alien to the typical acidic dourness of these high boggy flows and their little bog-hole lochs. I had a distant recollection of hearing that china clay occurred when there were pockets of decayed felspar in granite.

We stooped and prodded and turned over stones and rummaged excitedly among the weeds and reeds, and everywhere we found insects and larvae and shrimps and hog-lice and snails, a cornucopia of aquatic life to rival that of any Hampshire chalk stream. Here, by some freak of geology, was a little zone of astonishing richness and fertility in the midst of a high plateau of granite overlaid with acidic blanket peat. Fumbling with eager haste, we produced the little screw-top specimen bottles we had brought, and began collecting samples of the sand, the kaolin-like sediments, the larvae and crustaceans, and in an attempt to be at least slightly systematic we tried to remember to mark their labels against a roughly pencilled sketch map of the loch, so each specimen could be cross-referenced to the place where we had found it. Simplest of all, but potentially the most revealing, were the three samples we took of the water: not like china tea with suspended flecks of peat and grit, like the other lochs, but star-bright and brilliantly clear.

As for those legendary trout we had been told about, fishermen's tales are usually tiresome to non-fishers and liable to be dismissed as nothing more than exaggerated wishful thinking. Suffice it to say that we fished with silent dedication for almost five hours, while the setter made occasional questing forays in the heather, or lay with heaving flanks and flecked pink tongue and basked in sybaritic bliss on a patch of sun-warmed sand — and we caught three trout. All were over two pounds, and the best was a shade over $3^1/_2$. The average for the other lochs was about six ounces. We never saw a feeding fish break the surface, despite a continuous hatch of insects that on any other hill loch would have had the surface awash with the splashings of rising trout. The fishes' stomach contents told their own stories, each packed with invertebrate foods that had been eaten on the bottom or intercepted in mid-water. Why waste energy rising to emergent duns on the potentially dangerous sunlit surface when you could cruise in the cooler depths and feed at leisure on this *smorgasbord* of shrimps and snails and creeping larvae? These were sleek trout, deep in the flank and with a powerful hunch of muscle across the shoulders, silvery-olive above and with bellies a buttery gold, their sides spangled with a sparse scattering of black and carmine spots, looking like a totally different species compared with the typical blunt-headed dwarfishness of their dark-coloured neighbours in the other lochs of these hills. We had just over eight pounds weight of fish in the bass of woven rushes when we tried these three on the scales at home, and that was after several hours in which they would have lost some weight from drying out. From the other lochs a basket of twenty typical trout would probably have weighed slightly less.

The setter must have thought we had lost all interest in her tireless work, for she located two coveys of grouse and another scattering of snipe on the way back, without either of us paying much attention to her or the birds. Every long-distance motorist has occasionally found himself at his destination with little clear impression of the journey just driven, when his thoughts have been on other things. Our boggy, heathery miles back across the plateau and down to the car passed like that, almost unnoticed, for our thoughts were still at that loch, or on the little bottles of samples that clinked dully in our bags, where we had wrapped them in jerseys and stowed them. Two days later a more professional packaging of polystyrene and cardboard carried them off to the laboratories of a distant university, to a friend there who could analyse and verify their contents. And within another two days there came the anticipated rush of phone calls. Where had we found these? Were they all from the same water? If so, where was it? They simply *had* to know, since the water and clay samples were richer than any recorded from that north-western region, and the invertebrate specimens confirmed the presence of an environment of exceptional richness.

But we did not tell them then; and I am not going to reveal the secret now. Exposure and publicity and exploitation would surely ruin that little corner of magical richness, the bright and unsuspected jewel in the toad's head of those forbidding hills. Its secret is best kept among the small freemasonry of those who know and love it. Yet you may find it someday, too, if you try hard enough to earn it, for its little patch of blue and its ethereal Gaelic name are marked on the map for all to see, but looking no different on paper from the scores of other little lochs that are scattered across those wide expanses of heather and rock.

The Fish Hawk that Came Back

In 1986 a publisher friend asked me to write an Introduction to a new edition of an old and classic book on wildlife and sport, with one of those short and snappy titles beloved of nineteenth century publishers — *Short Sketches of the Wild Sports and Natural History of the Highlands*, first published in 1845, and written by Charles St. John. It is a celebrated book, one of the first to give a detailed account of Highland wildlife based on the author's personal observations, and it deserves to stay in print. But the mere mention of the author's name can cause teeth to grind and blood pressures to rise in fury, among at least some modern conservationists. For Charles St. John was one of those who saw and studied — and shot — the last of Britain's ospreys, and for that his name is inscribed forever on the blacklist of British natural history.

In fact, we need to see St. John in perspective, in the context of his age. He behaved in a way that was entirely typical of his age, and of the landowning and sporting class to which he belonged. Leisure and independent means, combined with a residence in the Highlands, gave him ample opportunities to see wildlife and enjoy fishing and shooting, and the ethos of the age was 'what's hit is history, what's missed is mystery'. Rare and interesting specimens were bagged with the gun, not 'shot' with a camera or filmed on video tape, and an enormous amount of what we now know about the world's birds and beasts was first brought to scientific attention by the collecting guns and killing bottles and traps of the Victorian explorers and sportsmen. The Highlands' ospreys and sea eagles were already on a steady slide towards extinction long before Charles St. John was born, owing to changing habitat and land use, compounded by widespread persecution by gamekeepers, and it is less than fair to lay all the blame for their eventual disappearance at one man's feet.

But his great achievement, for which he deserves full credit, was to publish an acutely observed and intimately detailed account of the wildlife of the north of Scotland in the years before the region was fully opened up by the new railways, and before the Victorian exploitation of Scotland as a sporting and recreational venue had got underway. Before putting pen to paper I got down my old copy of the book to re-read it, and I packed it to read in odd moments on a summer fishing trip to Invernesshire and Morayshire, which, quite by chance, was to include one or two places which Charles St. John had visited on his own travels 150 years or so earlier.

Since they first reappeared and tried to nest in Scotland in 1954, succeeding eventually in 1959, the ospreys of Speyside have become famous, especially at Loch Garten, where there are special well-advertised facilities for observing their favourite nesting tree. This set-up was a shrewd move, heightening the public's awareness of the return of a rare and spectacular breeding raptor, and also focussing all their interest on one nest site, thereby distracting attention from other nesting pairs and helping to minimise human disturbance at nesting time. There had been problems, including egg thieves and vandals, but the Loch Garten birds were to some extent expendable, a showpiece that occasionally suffered so that other ospreys could nest and become established in peace. By the late 1980s an estimated seventy pairs were known to be nesting in the Highlands. And some were in the Findhorn valley, the much loved haunt of Charles St. John in the 1830s, which happened to be my destination for a week's fishing. It would be a pleasant irony if I should be lucky enough to glimpse an osprey there during my visit.

A week later I was in Morayshire, on a cloudy day of squally rain, driving north-eastwards from Carrbridge across Dava Moor and past the bleak grey waters of Lochindorb and its island castle of the Wolf of Badenoch, the clan chieftain who held the area in thrall in medieval times. My destination was a few miles further on down the valley of the Findhorn, that magical Highland river that rises in the heart of the Monadliath hills and flows north-east to the sea just beyond Forres, its path almost parallel to the larger and more famous Spey to the east. Taking a minor road that swings northwards towards Cawdor and Nairn, I came to the bridge at Dulsie, where a soaring single arch of grey stone spans one of the Findhorn's deepest gorges; and there I found myself right in one of the scenes from St John's book. It happened to be 6 August, my birthday, and also the same date on which Charles St. John had first visited the Findhorn.

To illustrate *Wild Sports* St. John had been assisted by Charles Whymper, one of the principal wildlife and landscape illustrators of the period, and he contributed six engravings of scenes from the Findhorn valley, one of which is a dramatic picture of Dulsie Bridge, the gorge with its grey slabs of rock, and the dark, peat-stained waters of the Findhorn flowing underneath. I stopped the car and got out to peer over the parapet of the bridge — fishermen always look over bridges — and tried to imagine how the scene might have changed since St. John's visit. Hardly at all: apart from the tarmac road and a few road signs, he would have found it all quite familiar.

My host's little lodge lay a few miles further on, and it was not until after supper that we paid a quick visit to the river, to see the state of the water and whet our appetites for the first of the fishing next morning. The sky had cleared, the rain had gone, and there was a hint of warmth in the air — and more than a few midges, too. We startled two roe deer, a buck and a doe, among some low birches near the river, and they bounded off with a series of gruff barks and a bobbing of white tails, stopping suddenly about a hundred yards ahead of us and staring back, their foxy-red summer coats glowing brilliant in the golden light of the low evening sun. Then one barked again, and they were off for good this time, quickly lost to sight among tall bracken and willow bushes.

Over breakfast we checked the map of our fishing beat and agreed which pools each of us should fish first. Half an hour later I was unclipping my rod from the car-top clamps and making my way to the head of the first pool. A narrow throat of fast water rushed between two jutting knobs of rock, then fanned out and slowed into a calmer flow in the main body of the pool. I startled a dipper among the rocks, and it whizzed away upstream with a high *zit-zit* of indignation, straight as a dart on a blur of short wings.

If you are really concentrating on your fishing, your whole attention should be focussed on the water, your line and the workings of your fly. Perhaps the best results are achieved by salmon fishers who are just not interested in the other wildlife of the river, or who have the ability to switch off from all distractions. I am neither. So when the reflection of a large bird swept across the water I instinctively looked up, and saw something that almost made me lose balance and fall over backwards into the water.

It was an osprey, soaring not more than seventy or eighty feet above my head, and almost level with the tops of the trees on the farther bank. The underside of its wings and tail were a startling white, against which the darker markings contrasted strongly. It seemed to hang against the gentle downstream breeze, then swung gently to the left and drifted down the line of Scots pines, and from over their tops a second bird suddenly came into view. It glided on set wings to join the first one, and they soared together, the first bird slightly above the second, curling across the wind and back to pass almost directly above me. They were so close that even quite small details of plumage and coloration were easy to see, and so too was the difference in their sizes — a pair of adult ospreys, the male clearly a little smaller and a shade lighter in build than his mate, for this must surely be a breeding pair. Might they have nested nearby?

No sooner had the thought entered my head than confirmation appeared, in the form of three more ospreys, moving close together in a steady soaring glide from over the trees opposite, just where the male had appeared a few moments earlier. All five gathered into a loose formation and circled and glided above the river for the next ten minutes, never further than two hundred yards from me at any time. Then one of the young birds gave a few deep, languid flaps of its long slender wings and rose slightly, extending its legs and settling in one of the topmost branches of a pine on the opposite bank, a couple of hundred yards downstream from where I stood. Then another circled in to join it, while the others gently circled above and around them.

I decided to follow, winding in my line which by now was lying right downstream, with the fly firmly caught on an underwater rock. I twitched it clear, wound in, and pulled my small pair of binoculars out of their pocket in my fishing bag. A short distance down my side of the riverbank was a small grassy knoll, and I lay back against this and focussed the glasses on the birds. As if to provide the final proof that this was indeed a family that had been bred locally, they had led me right to the nest. High on the opposite bank was a Scots pine, set slightly apart from the others, and looking rather flat-topped by comparison. The binoculars' image showed that this was a broad nesting platform, a robust but ragged-looking horizontal arrangement of sticks and twigs and other debris, and two of the young birds were standing on top of it, one picking at something I couldn't see, the other gently extending and flexing its wings and occasionally letting the breeze lift it to hover briefly a few inches above the nest, then folding its wings and descending gently again. The others continued to drift in lazy sweeps around and above the tree, their soaring and gliding interrupted only occasionally by a few wing-flaps, deep and with a powerful and steady rowing action.

No trained and practised team of actors could have put on a better performance, allowing me to watch them at a distance of less than forty yards away across the river for most of the morning, staying at their posts while I ran to the car and fetched my camera, and still perching and circling while I changed a succession of lenses and shot off almost three rolls of film. It was a magnificent display, spectacular and wholly absorbing.

A distant voice attracted my attention, and I turned to see one of our party back beside the car. He shouted again, something I couldn't make out, but it had a questioning inflection. 'Five of them!' I called back. 'Five, just here!' and I turned back to the birds. Moments later there was an approaching clumping sound behind me, and a wader-clad figure appeared suddenly at my elbow. '*How many*?!' he demanded, puffing heavily with exertion. 'Did you say *five*? I haven't moved a fish all morning. Where are they, then?'

Jerked back to the serious reality of fishing, I apologised. 'Oh, d'you mean salmon? Sorry — I meant *ospreys*. Look!' and I pointed across to where the birds still perched and circled and flapped around their nesting tree. He gave me a look of bewilderment that turned to a mixture of relief and disbelief — relief that I had not in fact shown them up by catching five salmon when all the rest of the party had had a blank morning; and disbelief that I should be so excited by these birds. 'Come on, it's past lunch-time,' and he clumped off towards the car, while I bundled my kit together and followed. 'He's been at it again,' he grumbled as we stepped into the lunch hut 'McKelvie's been watching birds. Probably hasn't even had his line in the water,' and he bit contemptuously into a salad sandwich.

'Was it the ospreys, sir?' inquired the gillie, looking up from his task of touching up the points of some hooks with a small whetstone. 'Aye, they nested just by that pool where you started this morning.'

'Where he didn't start, you mean,' grumbled the sandwich muncher. 'I invited him here to catch fish, not look at birds!'

In the event, it turned out to be a week of few salmon and steadily falling water levels. But even Charles St. John had had his blank weeks in those generally salmon-rich years of the early nineteenth century, and I consoled myself (and tried with mixed success to console the others in our party) with the motto of the Flyfishers' Club — *Piscator non solum piscatur* — 'there is more to fishing than just catching fish'.

The Mushroom Mystery

About every third or fourth year there occurs some special combination of conditions — a cocktail of rainfall, humidity, warmth, patterns of livestock grazing — that gives us a bumper year for mushrooms and fungi of many kinds. The familiar field mushrooms are always welcome, and appear from July onwards. We make daily forays up the grassy pastures along the little river valley to collect each new day's crop that has appeared as if by magic overnight, white flecks studding the green like the biblical manna.

There was a time when mushrooms repelled me, an inevitable aversion brought on by a holiday job from school, when I had supplemented my pocket money by picking cultivated mushrooms, working like a troglodyte in perpetual Stygian darkness in the humid depths of great sheds, with only candlelight to see by. Several years had to pass before I could again look a mushroom squarely in the face. And in any case, the late summer and autumn collecting of field mushrooms and other wild edible fungi is fun, and bears no resemblance to that miserable routine of picking those comparatively tasteless cultivated versions.

I am curious about fungi, but still cautious, a national trait in the British Isles. Compare our tentative mistrust with the eager and knowledgeable enthusiasm of the French and the Italians, and other Europeans too, who make weekly family forays into their forests to collect fungi, usually on Sundays. In France it is a family ritual, with everyone *en fête* and heading for those great state forests that date from feudal times, that post-revolutionary France has nevertheless preserved so beautifully, with their good roads, their scattered *carrefour* clearings, each named or numbered, from which radial rides dissect the forest into segments. Here the French delight in systematic orderliness was originally applied to the practical business of keeping track of the hunted deer or boar and the pursuing hounds and riders. At any moment you might hear the distant, plangent call of a *trompe* blown to signal the progress of the hunt, and glimpse the passing of the fleeing quarry and the riders in thigh boots and tricorne hats, a Bourbon pageant brought to life, as still happens all over France. Herds of red deer, families of roe, and sounders of wild boar still roam these vast woods and are hunted with a ritual and style that would make any pre-guillotine aristocrat feel quite at home. The straight rides that radiate from the *carrefours* still perform the useful function of allowing the hunt follower to see the stag, or roebuck, or boar as it breaks across ahead of the hounds, and so to keep abreast of the hunt that is otherwise concealed among the trees.

The Gallic hunt for ceps and chanterelles, morells and boletus, is also conducted with skill and an instinctive kind of knowledge handed down from earlier generations. In a predominantly rural, agricultural society few French families are more than a generation or two away from the land and its heritage of country understanding. Grandparents wise in the lore of fungi still teach their children's children what to gather and what to avoid, for the French fungi hunt is an all-age, family affair. And to assist in doubtful cases, the pharmacies stay open specially on Sundays, to help identify the edible and eliminate the poisonous.

Early one October we were in the forest of Compiègne to the north-east of Paris, when we encountered an elderly woman delving for fungi among the undergrowth and leaf litter, and wielding a large and fierce-looking old bayonet with a blade about eighteen inches long as her digging implement — an unnecessarily powerful one for the task, we thought. As always in France we stopped and exchanged the little verbal courtesies that are almost unknown between strangers in modern Britain. Yes, it was indeed a fine day — and what of her fungi hunting? Yes, that was going well. 'And that is a fine bayonet you have, madame,' we remarked, a little doubtfully. 'Yes, a useful bayonet for digging up fungi,' she agreed. 'And for killing Englishmen!' she added with a loud cackle, her face split with a wide and broken-toothed grin, as she swung the blade upwards and flourished it above her head. Shades of the fierce *tricoteuses* at the guillotine, perhaps? We smiled ingratiatingly and withdrew to our car. 'Englishmen' forsooth! And us with nothing but pure Scots and Irish blood in our veins!

Like most Britons I began by being a little conservative about fungi, sticking to those readily identifiable as mushrooms and dismissing everything else as 'toadstools' and therefore probably tasteless at best, and possibly poisonous, perhaps even lethal. This over-cautious attitude, our national fungal bigotry, was reversed in the course of a woodland walk in autumn with a Wiltshire expert, Norwegian by birth, who had an encyclopedic grasp of fungi and their culinary properties. She had picked up her expertise through necessity, during the Nazi occupation of Norway when she was a child, when her family's meagre rations had been augmented by whatever wild foods they could find, including fungi in the autumn woods. Against such a background, first of harsh necessity and later of genuine enjoyment, the British conservatism that shuns most fungi must have seemed to her like a combination of ignorance and wasteful luxury.

In the British Isles we lack the wonderful richness of the great European forests of broadleafed trees growing on fertile lowland soils, which are sources of innumerable edible species of fungi. Our upland plantations of serried ranks of sitka spruce offer little excitement for the fungi hunter, although larch is something of an exception to most of the commercially-grown species of conifers, and can repay some exploration, especially where the larch stands are broken up with native species like birch. The fringes of these forestry blocks tend to be best, the rides and firebreaks and the unplanted river margins, where willow and birch and rowan and the occasional rugged Scots pine grow at random. Mixed deciduous woodlands with a good mixture of tree species and ages are always interesting for fungi, provided they are not growing on very alkaline soils.

Some of the most profuse and varied growths of fungi I have even encountered in Britain were in mixed plantations of birch, ash, lodgepole pine, spruce and Scots pine in north-east Sutherland in the wet August of 1992, that followed a long dry spell from spring to late summer. Chanterelles, ceps and boletus had done especially well, and covered the woodland floor in profusion wherever we looked. At home there was a rich crop, too, with the ceps particularly abundant under the old beeches, on the fringes of fields grazed all summer by sheep. But it was a daily battle against the continuing wet weather, as the moisture invited a continual invasion of the fungi by snails, slugs and insects, reducing many to a mushy pulp before we could find and pick them. The local and individual variations were innumerable, too, and for a couple of weeks the field guide lay open and was subjected to repeated thumbings as we checked our finds against its entries and pictures. Dumfriesshire chemists do not yet offer a consultancy service to amateur mycologists.

Prowlers in the Half-Light

A late supper with friends meant it was just gone 1am when we turned in off the road and down the drive towards the house. In the headlights was the shape of a badger, greyish-brown in the glare of the main beam. She — it appeared to be a medium-sized sow — swung away from us and started off downhill on the tarmac at a steady trot, trundling along with a sailor's rolling gait ahead of us, her grey coat overhanging her flanks and almost brushing the ground like a shaggily-fringed pelmet, and quite determined not to be unduly hustled by this curious glaring monster that had suddenly interrupted her night's prowling. We slowed and followed at a respectful distance as she trundled steadily along, almost as if she might any moment mutter over her shoulder a testy reminder that 'steam gives way to sail'. She plodded purposefully, showing no signs of leaving the illuminated strip of driveway for the safety of the grass verges or the anonymity of the dark fields to either side, until just twenty yards short of the house she jinked sideways and slid off into the gloom in the general direction of the stables and the large sett that lies beyond at the bottom of the lower fields.

Perhaps she just waited in the dark until we had gone indoors before resuming her wanderings; or perhaps she came back later, in the early hours, maybe even with other badgers; or perhaps she simply left some particularly prominent scent markings behind her. Whatever the reason, before breakfast some six hours later the dogs tumbled out and made straight for the driveway, all on the scent of something especially interesting, their tails held high and stiff, their noses making a meticulous examination of the grass and the gravel. They seldom fail to detect the aftermath of nocturnal badger and fox activity, and their morning behaviour alerts us to what has been going on in the night. From February to July there is a well-travelled badger and fox trail that cuts right across our fields, and both use it constantly, presumably aware of the house routine and knowing when the dogs are safely indoors and out of their way.

A colony of badgers has lived for as long as anyone locally can remember under the old beeches that line the rim of the river gorge, coexisting in apparent harmony with at least two families of foxes that share the same extended labyrinth of tunnels under the tangled tree-roots, among the sandy soil and the loose underlying shale. The setting is worthy of an Arthur Rackham painting, with the long, half-exposed roots spreading down the bank like smooth tentacles. The combined comings and goings of the badgers and foxes have worn a clear track along the lip of the precipice, a well-trodden path that provides their main approaches to the sett and earths from east and west, just out of sight behind the fence and among the little self-sown beech saplings.

The foxes make their presence all too apparent, barking and skirling in the still of frosty winter nights, sometimes right under our bedroom window; taking the occasional bantam from our little flock of millefleurs; sometimes wandering unconcernedly about the fields and even across the lawns in full view in the summer and late autumn; and forever tainting the air with the hot, rank smell of fox that drives the dogs into frenzied ecstacies of barking. And they specialise in depositing their scats along the grassy edges of the drives, just to ensure that the dogs don't have to quest too far next morning to find something really irresistibly nasty to roll in.

By comparison the badgers are the souls of discretion and unobtrusive privacy. On summer evenings they slip up from the sett to root about with silent dedication among the primroses, the wild garlic and the snowdrop bulbs on the grassy bank behind the stables, choosing their times with care, when dogs and people are safely indoors and the coast is clear. When the wind is favourable and we can move undetected into position behind the straggly low beech hedge, we peer over and watch them as they systematically hoover their way along the little terraces of the slope below. Noses grub and front paws scrabble with single-minded energy as they work their slow way along the bank, wholly absorbed in the hunt for delicacies, but still alert to the slightest alien sound. A scrunch of gravel, an incautious footfall, a clink of loose change in one's pocket, and they are all ears, heads up and noses twitching in alarm, and then off downhill at such speed that we expect any moment to see them take a tumble and roll headlong. It must be their very low centre of gravity that enables them to keep on an even keel in their downhill rush. Once down the hill and on the flat pasture they still maintain a surprising turn of speed until they have reached the cover of the beeches and the familiar security of home.

The badgers make good neighbours, and we try to repay the compliment, looking on them as a major asset. There have been occasional rumours of badger diggers raiding setts not far away, apparently in search of animals to be spirited off in sacks and rushed down the nearby motorway to illegal baiting pits in the Midlands. So we keep an eye open for strange cars parked anywhere near the river, for unfamiliar figures crossing the fields or walking in the vicinity, especially if they are accompanied by dogs. The hunt earth-stoppers pose no threat, appearing early on one or two winter mornings to stop the entrances when the foxhounds are meeting nearby, and returning before dusk to open them up again. When hounds are in the vicinity probably the badgers' safest place is well underground in temporary confinement, so the earth-stoppers have done them a favour.

Like the badgers, the sea trout fishers like to be abroad in the long gloamings of summer evenings. When local expertise judges that the water conditions are just right, they park their cars along the quiet by-road and slip down to the river, to cast a fly as the trout come up to the evening rise, or to trundle a worm down the pool as dusk gathers and the first of the sea trout come on the move. Careful, dedicated fishing takes too much concentration for the fishers to see much of the shadowy creatures that slip by in the half-light; that privilege is reserved for those who sit and wait silently, perhaps gently puffing a pipe or smoking a cigarette to keep the midges away, and waiting for the critical time when it's best to start fishing. Then, if they keep still and the wind is in their favour, they can see badgers emerge and move across the meadows, and maybe even glimpse an otter as he begins his night's fishing. Night fishing for sea trout is another world, an affair of magnified sounds and mysterious shadows, of animal and bird calls unknown by daylight, and may include the sudden appearance of a badger rummaging at your very feet on the riverbank, a quick moonlit encounter with a chunky body and a silver-striped head as each of you startles the other.

The foxes are on the move at dusk, too. In summer they often lie up and bask by day in clearings in the gorse on the river banks, but as the sun dips and the light thickens they are off on their nightime journeyings. Silent shapes of richest red slip across the pastures, seldom in a hurry, often pausing to listen and sniff the air, sometimes sitting down and

scratching like a dog, yet never aimless. They seem to move purposefully, as if their routes had been planned carefully in advance.

It is seldom that we hear any sounds from foxes in late spring or summer, unless it is the squeaks and thin yappings of young cubs tumbling and romping in play near the mouth of their earth. Winter is the time when the long hours of darkness conceal them from sight, yet that is when their screams and barkings are clearly audible almost nightly. Frosty nights of clear cold air seem to trigger off volleys of vulpine barkings and shriekings. It sometimes seems as though foxes like the sound of their own voices, and bark and skirl just for the sake of it, like singing in the bath. Or perhaps those are simply the conditions which the foxes like best, when they can hear one another most clearly and often at considerable distances. Or perhaps it is just that human ears can hear them best on nights when all sounds travel far and clear. I have often heard foxes calling on nights of heavy rain, and have sometimes been jolted into startled wakefulness by foxes screaming right under my bedroom window on dark nights with mist and heavy drizzle. But there is something especially wild and exciting about the calls of foxes on the crisp air of a still and freezing night in midwinter, as their voices echo to and fro across the little river valley. A white hoar frost or a light powdering of snow is even better, especially if there is a moon, for then the elusive shapes of dog foxes and vixens can often be seen as dark silhouettes against the silvery background as they slip about the fields and over the pastures that fringe the stream. In more exotic parts of the world I have heard wolves howling by night, but there is something just as wild and spine-tingling and primeval in the winter sounds of mating foxes.

But for some reason I could not fathom, one particular vixen suddenly became especially vocal in summer. Her most conspicuous display came one warm sunny evening in late July, when I was sitting working at my study desk, the window open and my view dominated by the two horses that were standing, nose to tail and motionless except for their ceaseless tail-swishings at the inevitable flies. I turned reluctantly back to the computer screen and was soon absorbed in the questionable delights of doing my VAT accounts. Then a sharp, shrill scream jerked me back to the real world outside. It came from somewhere close by, the unmistakeable shrieking skirl of a vixen, high and long drawn out. From the dogs, all shut indoors, there was an answering burst of furious barking, the high yapping of the terrier mingling with the sharp collie-like barks of the lurcher and the more orotund baritones of the labradors and the setter. That should scare her off, I thought, as I dashed to the front door, hoping for at least a glimpse of a departing fox.

Then it came again, the same spine-tingling scream, even closer this time, and apparently from just beyond the lawn and the garden hedge, no more than forty yards away. There was the same answering canine pandemonium from indoors, a volley of uncontainable fury. Nothing seemed to move in the first field beyond the hedge, yet when the next scream came it was from further off to my left. The vixen was on the move, though I could not see her yet. Grabbing binoculars, I moved to a spot that gave me a good view of all three fields that surround the house, and I waited. Another scream, long and sustained, and this time I had a good fix on the direction. Nothing showed in the binoculars except a clump of docks and thistles — and then the fox appeared.

She was slim and sleek and elegant, a slender young vixen, and probably one of last year's cubs. She walked slowly across to my right, stopping and walking again several times until she reached another tuft of thistles. Then she threw her head up and screamed again, long and loud and anguished. Another ten or twelve seconds without movement, and then she was off again, circling right-handed and moving slowly. At the hedgerow by the drive she paused and seemed to wait and listen, then screamed again, and was lost to sight in the narrow belt of thick summer undergrowth. A few moments later she was out in the open again, crossing the tarmac slowly and then halting at the edge of the little pond, then slipping on through another hedge and into the lower field.

By now I was looking directly down onto her, barely twenty yards below me and standing quite still beside a wooden feeding trough left since the lambs had been fed there. Again she seemed to listen and wait, then sat down gently and threw her head back in another piercing screech; then another spell of waiting and listening, and then another slow walk down the field.

For almost half an hour she circled the house, slipping steadily from field to field, always stopping at some little feature like a thistle clump or a hedge or a boulder, screaming continually, and then moving on clockwise. Another full circuit, punctuated with stops and screams, and then she melted away, finally lost to sight as she slipped through the thick line of bushes that fringes the slope above the river.

Why a vixen circling and screaming in broad daylight in July? This activity was what I associate with winter, cold and darkness, when the skirling of a vixen often comes out of the blackness and is repeated again and again as she makes a circuit of the fields, calling as she goes, and often answered by the high, crisp barking of a dog-fox in the distance. Perhaps this was an unmated vixen, calling in the forlorn hope of summoning a mate in high summer. Or was it a breeding fox that had lost her cubs or her mate? I never discovered, nor could I find anyone to give me a convincing explanation of her curious behaviour.

To see foxes here in Dumfriesshire, or in almost any other rural area, is a common enough event, especially at dawn and dusk, or by night. To encounter one after a long day of tedious meetings in London, followed by a late dinner with friends, was less expected. The roads around Wandsworth, like city roads everywhere, are bathed by night in a bilious yellow street lighting that washes out most other hues. Even the brightest primary colours merge into an indeterminate grey overlaid with sodium yellow, except for all but the brightest neon lights in shops and the cowled lamps of the traffic lights. Driving south alongside Wandsworth Common just after midnight on a cold, dry February night, I slowed as a low, scampering shape emerged from the scrubby hedgerow to my right. Another cat on the prowl, probably, risking one of its lives by dashing across the road. But no, it trailed a long and heavy tail, and then stopped stock still, pricked ears cocked — a fox.

And then another, that started out from the shadows of the same hedge-line and came across the road at a steady trot. It paused near the centre of the road to inspect a piece of litter that lay there, probably a discarded hamburger bag or a kebab wrapper. Its partner trotted up to join it, and the two then meandered off up the line of cat's-eyes that stretched ahead along the crown of the road. I edged the car forwards slowly, and they swung to the left, mounting the pavement and wandering along it with all the insouciance of two stray dogs left out for the night, their gaunt shapes meagre and unkempt-looking. More litter on the pavement detained them as they inspected it for a moment, one of them picking something up in its mouth and carrying it a few paces before dropping it: they didn't even look up as I accelerated past. Less than three hundred yards further on there was yet another fox on the pavement, bigger this time, but with the same attenuated thinness of the others, its scrawny tail dragging low.

The invasion of suburbia by foxes seems sad, for it so often means that we see a magnificent wild mammal in a miserable state, the alert, lithe, full-coated vitality of the country fox transformed into a scraggy scavenger of alleys and back gardens, eking out an existence among litter bins and the discarded sandwich papers in urban parks. Perhaps it has its own interest for specialist fox watchers, who see a rural species steadily colonising the towns and cities, and finding a niche in the heart of the densest human settlements. Perhaps it is a modern object lesson in how wild creatures can adopt man as a source of food and shelter and survival, just as cats and dogs once adopted humans. (Only the vanity and arrogance of mankind could make us think that it was we who made the first moves to domesticate *them*.) But those cringing, shadowy spectres dependent on the scraps they could find on London streets appeared such a travesty of their true selves, the glowing red foxes of the woods and fields and hills, that live cavalier bandit lives, shrinking from human contact and thriving best when every man's hand is turned against them. They might be quite another species, those big foxes of the northern woods and the heather moors, setting man at defiance in their bold independence, not foraging in his debris like rats.

Foraging comes naturally to foxes, which are opportunist feeders, and happy to pick up whatever unconsidered trifles may have been left about. In the Scottish Border country there has been a marked increase in fox numbers since the late 1980s, a trend which I am sure has been promoted by a succession of mild winters and good summers, and also the decline and fall of the traditional livestock knackery trade. Thanks to various new European edicts and regulations, fallen stock are not now collected and taken away from farms by professional knackers, and the hunts are also more restricted in what they can take from farms as flesh for the hounds. Farmers now have to dispose of their own dead stock, usually by burying, and some do this more diligently and efficiently than others.

Inevitably, there is now a great deal more carrion, especially sheep and lambs, left lying about the countryside and affording a ready source of good feeding for foxes, and other carrion feeders, too, including crows, stoats, buzzards and badgers. All seem to be thriving, especially in areas where there are large acreages of commercial conifer

plantations, which are seldom subject to any systematic control of predatory species, unlike conventionally keepered woodland and farms. And the foxes have benefitted mightily, with good feeding to ensure that they come through the mild winters in excellent condition, with fertile vixens rearing sturdy litters of cubs in spring, and a higher than usual proportion of the cubs surviving to full maturity and breeding in their turn. Why forage far afield and expend time and energy searching for shrews and frogs and the occasional rabbit when there is abundant food close at hand? The result is smaller fox territories and a significant and steady increase in the population.

Deer for Tomorrow

'A damned sika! Those things are a menace! The worst possible introduction! They're destroying all our red deer!' The friend who uttered these words is not alone in his dislike of sika deer, though he expresses himself more forcefully than most. And misgivings about sika can stem from several causes, depending on your point of view. That particular conversation took place in Ireland, where there is a serious problem regarding the hybridisation of sika with red deer, a phenomenon that is not widespread in Great Britain, though it does occur. Many mammal enthusiasts look with dismay at the way in which the dwindling numbers of wild indigenous Irish red deer are threatened by hybridisation with burgeoning populations of sika, especially in Wicklow. It has even been argued that there are no entirely pure red deer to be found anywhere in those eastern counties.

Other considerations also arouse antagonism to sika. Purists deplore the way alien, introduced species can find an undreamed-of niche, sometimes proliferating at the expense of native species. The grey squirrel's spread and the native red squirrel's decline is perhaps the most frequently cited example of this. And sika have established thriving and expanding colonies in many parts of the British Isles, from Killarney and Dorset to Lancashire and Sutherland.

And then there are the foresters, at any rate those who were trained in the commercial forestry ethos of the 1960s and 1970s, who tend to detest any creatures that damage young trees — and sika are as good at this as any other deer. The more enlightened and realistic foresters of the 1990s realise that deer are an amenity that can provide aestheic pleasure, sporting enjoyment and revenue, and an income from selling the annual harvest of venison, to supplement the cash crop of timber, and to offset the relatively slight damage the animals do in well laid out and properly managed forests. And in any case it has proved virtually impossible either to eradicate deer by shooting, or to fence them out of new plantations, and they should therefore be regarded as just another site factor to be taken into account when planning and planting a new woodland.

I have watched sika-red deer hybrids in Ireland and the Kintyre region of Argyllshire, and they look ungainly and ugly compared with the elegant majesty of red deer and the compact integrity of pure sika, 'the little deer of Nippon'. The general policy of shooting all hybrids seems wise, although things may already have gone too far to rescue the pure red deer population of eastern Ireland from extinction through hybridisation.

What causes hybridisation is still unclear, and many populations of red and sika deer coexist happily without any signs of cross-breeding. In the New Forest, for example, you can see reds and sika mingling and sharing the same habitat, and the same in Dorset, where wild and park deer of both species retain their genetic purity. Yet there has been hybridisation in Lancashire. Physically, the obvious liaison is between a red deer hind and a sika stag, and perhaps mating occurs when a wandering sika stag moves into red deer range and encounters a red hind in season.

One of my favourite western forests holds a sizeable herd of pure Japanese sika, introduced by the local landowning family in the 1880s, when they, like so many estate owners, were members of the enthusiastic Acclimatisation Society that sought to establish wildlife from other lands in British habitats. The Viscount Powerscourt at Powerscourt in

Wicklow, Sir Victor Brooke at Colebrook, and the Duke of Abercorn at Baronscourt all introduced sika to their Irish estates, obtaining most of their stock from the celebrated Carl Jamrach, a London-based dealer in exotic animals. On all three estates they have thrived subsequently, although escapees from Powerscourt are blamed for the hybridisation with red deer in surrounding areas of Wicklow and south County Dublin. (Hybridisation was something of a feature of Lord Powerscourt's collection of animals, and included successful breeding from hybrids of wapiti or North American elk and red deer, something that also occurred at Caledon in County Tyrone, where the Earl of Caledon introduced a wapiti hind to his enclosed park herd of red deer.)

Our sika-watching expeditions are mainly dawn and dusk affairs, moving carefully on foot at first light to intercept deer retreating to the daytime cover of the woods after a night's feeding out on the surrounding open land, and watching from high seats on the woodland edge at dusk, as the deer become active and gradually emerge once again from among the trees. They drift in and out of cover like shadows in the poor light of dawn and dusk; and with even a large sika stag only standing breast high to a man, they are easily lost to sight among long vegetation and in even quite slight depressions and folds in the ground. Unless surprised, they are as quiet as shadows, too; but if we stumble upon a party of hinds, or if a tricky breeze should swirl our scent towards them, there comes a high *peep*-ing volley of little yelps as necks stretch and ears flick around for telltale sounds, before they turn tail and bound off for the safety of the treeline and the dark green woodland depths that lie within.

But their accustomed silence and furtive movements are quite abandoned, by the stags at least, when late September brings on the annual rutting time. Then a strange sound fills the woods and echoes off the hillsides, a weird and penetrating blast of sound that is like no other creature in the European countryside — the whistle of a rutting sika stag. Without warning, it may come as an earsplitting shock, a sustained ringing blast that sets unsuspecting nerves a-jangle in the dusky loneliness of a spruce forest.

It is quite different from the sustained, resonant, almost bovine roaring of a rutting red deer stag, and more akin to the unexpectedly high-pitched belling of North American elk. And all these are indeed closely related species — some have argued that they are in fact merely local variants of one widely varying deer species — that are found across a vast natural range in the northern hemisphere, from the elk of Canada and the USA to the red deer of northern Europe and Asia, and the smaller sika of eastern Asia, Manchuria, Japan and Taiwan.

Sika have a grumpy, disgruntled expression, especially the grizzle-faced stags, which is undoubtedly accentuated by the prominent V-shaped pattern of raised bones on the animal's face. This ridge-faced appearance can be seen quite prominently in some other eastern deer, too, including the massive sambar of India, and especially in the heavily-ridged mask of the little muntjac, now such a common and increasing species in southern and central England. But my experiences of sika seem to indicate that they tend to be quite aggressive and short-tempered by nature, and not just in appearance.

Stags, especially young and middle-aged beasts, will fight readily and angrily over territorial disputes and at rutting time, and along woodland rides in sika country I have often seen the ground strewn with tufts of hair that the deer have bitten out of each others' coats in their tussles.

Perhaps their introduction to Britain, like other ill-considered enthusiasms of the Victorian acclimatisers, was not altogether wise. But hindsight is a luxury that today's naturalists and wildlife managers cannot afford, and we start from where we are, with a responsibility to husband our herds of sika, and of other non-native deer, alongside the red deer and the roe that colonised by a natural westward drift after the icesheets uncovered these islands ten millenia ago.

The undoubted problems of sika-red hybridisation is a minor matter compared to the other management challenges that deer present us with in the 1990s. Roe, formerly confined to the south of England, the far north, and Scotland, are steadily colonising the south-west and East Anglia, the Midlands and across the Severn into Wales, presenting problems for farmers, foresters and gardeners as they go. Muntjac, the little barking deer of south-east Asia that escaped from Woburn and became a successful feral species, are steadily spreading across most of central and southern England, and may soon be the commonest of all the six species of deer at large in the wild in Britain.

But the greatest challenge and the most heated controversy has focussed on the red deer of Scotland, the unique population of comparatively small red deer that have adapted to a bleak life on the open hills of the Highlands. A combination of factors, including afforestation, new philosophies of land management, and changing sporting practices, have led to a population explosion among the Highland deer, with 1992 numbers estimated at over 300,000 animals, over double the total of twenty years earlier. Those who are wise in the ways of deer have recognised the need to reduce total red deer numbers, to minimise deer damage in woodland and on farmland, and to maintain a healthy and well-balanced population. Others, less familiar with deer but shrill and opinionated and highly vociferous in the press and on radio and television, have raised an outcry about alleged deer damage, and have almost managed to turn public opinion against the largest and most impressive land mammal in Britain, which was always hitherto respected as the monarch of the glens. Between autumn 1992 and February 1993 an unprecedentedly large cull of around 60,000 deer took place on Scottish estates, and Nature seems to have further assisted the cull in her own way, to judge from the unusually low pregnancy rates among hinds after the 1992 rut. A stable population of about 170,000 red deer seems within sight by the mid 1990s.

However, the general controversy appears set to continue about the role of red deer in the ecology of the Highlands. Properly managed in the traditional ways that have always been practised on the best run-deer forests, deer can be the best of all food converters on the meagre fare of the Scottish hills, can provide a magnificent source of nutritious, low fat, well-flavoured meat free of all additives — the 'greenest' of all forms of flesh for the table — and can generate substantial revenue from sporting stalkers, in addition to their amenity value, which is delightful and impossible to evaluate in terms of pounds and pence.

Others, however, want to see deer numbers slashed — figures as low as 50,000 have been mentioned — to allow the natural birch scrub of the hills to regenerate, followed in the long term by the Scots pine that is the natural climax stage of Highland vegetation. This, they argue, will allow much of the Highlands to revert to its 'natural' state of several centuries ago, and will promote a greater range and diversity of woodland species of animals, plants, birds and insects. However, this argument seems to overlook the fact that Scotland's red deer were originally woodland animals, and that to exclude them from the recreated Scottish woods would be to omit an essential element in the Highland fauna, and the one that has more powerful aesthetic and commercial appeal than any other mammal. It is also based on the questionable assumption that people will wish to live and work, or to spend their holidays, in a landscape very different from that of the Highlands at present. The leagues of rolling heather and open hill country are the hallmark of the Highlands, and the red deer that live there are uniquely Scottish. Do we really wish to lose that in exchange for acres of birch scrub?

'If it pays, it stays' is a handy phrase often used by game conservationists in Africa, where wild game has an appreciable value for local economies. If only the British housewife could be persuaded to experiment with the unfamiliar delights of well-presented cuts of venison, a whole new market might emerge to allow venison to command a realistic price, in addition to the large sums that sportsmen are already willing to pay for red deer stalking on the hills. An unfortunate and ridiculous myth has been perpetuated that venison is somehow too gamey and exotic for ordinary tastes, requiring complex and sometimes bizarre methods of preparation and cooking. Nothing could be less true; and there are plenty of venison lovers who have never seen the inside of any of the exotic and expensive restaurants of London and European capitals.

Many a Highland crofter and hill farmer has a ready taste for red deer venison, and is not entirely displeased to see an occasional party of deer raiding his fields, perhaps slipping down from the hill or out of the woods as night falls on a winter's evening. He may make a fuss about the damage that deer do to his crops — and they can be a menace sometimes — but he will not be slow to dash out and shoot a couple of nice plump young hinds for his freezer. The rest of the herd will scatter in alarm and either return to the hill or raid some other farmer's land — and there will be delicious venison for supper, cooked and served simply, all for the price of a couple of cartridges. 'A beast from the hill, a salmon from the river, and a grouse from the heather' have traditionally been claimed as every Highlander's entitlement, and although they may occasionally be poached, every realistic landowner recognises that this is a comparatively harmless local custom, and quite different from ruthless large-scale commercial poaching. What would be intolerable is the prospect of a massive cull of 100,000 beasts or more, perhaps to be carried out at public expense, to reduce red deer populations to a fraction of their traditional levels, and for the remnants to be confined in fenced parks, instead of enjoying a wholly free life on the hills.

Ice Age Legacies

A trout is a trout is a trout.' That is what most people interested in fish and fishing have been taught, at least for most of the past fifty years. A monster from a dark loch, a speckled dark brownie from a hill stream, a noble two-pounder from a Hampshire chalk stream, a streamlined silver ingot fresh in on the tide to a Welsh river or a Connemara lough — all are members of the richly varied family of *salmo trutta*, that will interbreed happily when mixed in a fish-farm, producing fertile stock. *Ergo* one species - simple, isn't it? We have been taught to think of trout as being rather like dogs, varying from the Great Dane to the Chihuahua, or like mankind itself, from pygmy bushman to Nordic giant, exhibiting a vast range of styles, sizes, colours and physical types, but all just manifestations of a single all-embracing species. 'Plastic' and 'polymorphic' are the technical terms that spring lightly to the lips of biologists when confronted with such variable creatures.

It was not always so. The game fishermen and fisheries experts of Victorian times examined trout from scores of rivers and hundreds of lochs across Britain, and from continental waters too, and then categorised innumerable distinct species of trout. *Salmo* was their common family name, but what a profusion of local types and physical forms, classified as separate species. The black-finned trout of the Welsh mountain tarns were *nigripinnis*, the thick-stomached snail- and shrimp-eating trout of Scottish and Irish lochs were *stomachicus*, the migrant sea trout was *fario* or *eriox*, and the silvery darlings of Loch Leven were *levenensis*, while in the dark depths of glaciated lakes from Cumberland to Sutherland and Galway cruised the massive *ferox*, the heavy-jowled cannibal trout that haunts so much of nineteenth century fishing literature.

The exuberant new mood of the scientific world after Darwin encouraged a penchant for multiplying the diversity of species. The taxonomic splitters were eagerly at work, subdividing old groupings of creatures into a plethora of new species, based on local variations of coloration, size, behaviour and diet, and revelling in the belief that natural selection and evolution had led to a diversity never before imagined.

Most pendulum swings of fashion, in science as in everything else, are followed by almost equal and opposite tendencies, and the splitters were soon followed by the 'lumpers'. A new generation of fish biologists began to retrench in their classifications, dismissing many alleged species as nothing more than local variants; and so began the return to the one-trout views of earlier times and of more recent orthodoxy.

If fishing is a disease, an addiction which is probably incurable and lifelong, if not directly life-threatening, then I can identify the precise moment of my infection. I was seven years old, I longed to catch a fish, and I came under the kindly tutelage of a retired Irish parson, who loved his fishing. He gave me my first rod, took me to catch my first trout — all of five ounces, from a hill lough — and fuelled some latent instinct to be a flyfisher. Even at that age, it was soon obvious to me that one trout could look very different from another. But why? How come that one little lake held tiny, blunt-headed fish with blood red spots while another, barely a mile away over the heather, was full of streamlined silvery trout with only a spangling of black speckles? And on the bigger waters, why did some trout I caught look so different from the others from the very same loch? I wanted to know more.

Back at school, in the endless weeks of winter terms, the lochs of summer were a world away. But there were books about fish in the library. Some forgotten old boy had left his *alma mater* a wonderful collection of old books on wildlife and sport, and on grey afternoons when I'd managed to escape the muddy hooliganism of house rugby there were hours of delight, perching on the warmth of a massive cast-iron radiator and leafing through those books about fish by experts with imposing names like Gunther and Regan, Jardine and Grimble. From their pages tumbled a deluge of italicised Latin names of trout — *estuarius* for the trout of river estuaries, *orcadensis* from the brackish lochs of Orkney, *gallivensis* for the sea trout of Connemara, *albus* and *brachypoma* for the sea trout of eastern

English and Scottish coasts, but *cambricus* for their Welsh cousins. My Latin master might have coaxed a better O-level pass out of me if he had taught us about Latin fish names, instead of the conventional conjugations and declensions. Where to begin? And could I possibly manage to catch just one of each kind, even if I lived to be a hundred?

By the late 1960s I was at university in Dublin, reading English, but spending perhaps too much of the spring term with a fishing rod in my hand. In a second-hand bookshop I found a battered copy of Day's *British and Irish Salmonidae* of 1887, its cover stained and many pages missing, but still with its brightly-coloured plates intact, revealing a rich and bewildering kaleidoscope of different coloured trout, salmon, grayling and char. At the south end of College Park was the zoological department, where J.R. Harris had compiled his celebrated *An Angler's Entomology* in the 1940s, and where my zoologist contemporaries drank coffee in an atmosphere reeking of formaldehyde and talked knowledgeably of genetics and the emerging techniques of genetic fingerprinting. I listened, baffled, and went fishing again, with Lough Melvin in north-west Ireland a special favourite. Here, for reasons neither the locals nor I could fathom, there were at least four types of trout, and possibly even five. And it was on Melvin that a team of freshwater biologists from Belfast's Queen's University undertook a study of the trout in the 1980s, and applied techniques of genetic analysis to the proteins in the fishes' blood and flesh.

Dr Andrew Ferguson and his colleagues proved what the Melvin fishermen had always suspected — that there are at least four distinct and genetically-discrete species of trout in the lough, all living and feeding and spawning in this one stretch of water, yet retaining their genetic purity and the distinctive physical appearance that enabled us to tell them apart.

Along the rocky shores and in the sandy bays live the *gillaroo*, Gaelic for the 'red fellow', and as superbly marked a trout as you could wish to see, with a belly of buttery gold, a powerfully muscular build, and a rich scattering of spots of deepest black and blood red. Shrimps and snails and other crustaceans comprise much of its diet, and the stomach wall is specially adapted, thick and muscular, to crush and grind this tough material. This is the *stomachicus* trout of the old splitters. It spawns in the sandy bays or drops down the single outflowing river to make redds and deposit its eggs in the gravel, well away from the spawning grounds of the other Melvin trout. To catch him you stalk the shoreline, or drift in close in a boat, casting your flies into the shallowest water along the margins of the lough where the *gillaroo* feed. The 'red fellow' may be so called because of the rich golden-red livery it assumes when autumn spawning is imminent, or because of his red flesh tinted by the carotene in his diet, or because of his crimson spots — or perhaps because of all three.

Melvin is deep, in a glaciated trench that drops to over two hundred feet in places, and it is out over the deeper water that you find another quite different trout, the *sonaghan*. They tend to live in shoals close to the surface, and are continually on the move, feeding actively on tiny zooplankton, especially *daphnia* or water fleas. Use a marrow scoop or a stomach siphon on a *sonaghan* and you will invariably find it has eaten a mass of little water fleas, and perhaps a mayfly or two in summer. Anyone could be forgiven for

assuming this to be a quite different species from the *gillaroo*, partly from its habitat but especially from its looks, and the genetic studies proved them correct. Barely a red spot here, except for a few small pinkish ones near the tail and below the lateral line, but there is a clear scattering of large black spots on the olive/gunmetal flanks and on the gill covers. Nor does the *sonaghan* reach the size of some *gillaroo*, which can run up to five or six pounds. Most *sonaghan* are about fourteen ounces, and anything over eighteen ounces is a trophy. The head is small and neat, the tail dark, square and massive, and all the fins are proportionately large and powerful, giving the *sonaghan* a fighting energy out of all proportion to its small size, and greater than that of any other trout I have encountered. They take the fly with a lightning smash and are gone at once if you don't tighten instantly, and their pectoral fins are unusually elongated and dark. Here is the splitters' *nigripinnis* — the dark-finned one. The old hands on Melvin used to say it was a landlocked sea trout, and it shares the sea trout's streamlined shape and power; but the lough has a clear link with the Atlantic just six miles from its western end, and salmon run up into it in every month of the year, so this is no landlocked water. (And for some unknown reason, this lough-and-river system receives no runs of sea trout, while all the neighbouring rivers do.) At spawning time, as at other periods of the year, the *sonaghan* have their own haunts, and lay their eggs in certain specific feeder streams where other trout do not spawn. They are the most abundant trout in the lough, numbering at least 200,000 fish over ten inches, according to a scientific survey, and in 1985 a team of 114 competitors in a flyfishing competition caught a total of 759 of them in a single day.

Cruise over Melvin's depths with a sonar fish-finder on your boat and you will pick up occasional large blips on the screen display, usually deep down and often surrounded by masses of smaller specks. These are the great *ferox* trout, cruising after the shoals of Arctic char they feed on, and often attaining weights of ten pounds and more. You'll see a few fine specimens in glass cases in houses and pubs around the lough, and the old books relate awesome tales of these massive trout, seldom the victims of flies fished near the surface, and usually taken by trolling in Melvin's deeper waters. A dark olive green, with

little spotting and a proportionately heavy head, the *ferox* type can be distinguished even in a tiddler of a few ounces, for it now seems that a *ferox* is born a *ferox*, and does not merely mature into a malevolent cannibal as it grows old, as was once thought. His kind spawn in just one of the feeder streams, and are often taken in the traps set for spawning salmon prior to the stripping of their eggs and milt for the hatchery.

Lough Melvin's fourth trout is distinct from all of the other three types, and conforms most closely to the typical brown trout that occur in most of the larger western waters of

Ireland and Scotland. Like the other three, it too reveals its own distinct genetic fingerprint when the magic of electrophoretic analysis is applied to its tissues.

Here is a challenge to any diehard adherents of the lumping theory of a one-species trout. Melvin has never been stocked — its trout population is so high that this has never been necessary — and its waters have been geographically isolated since the last ice age, with no links to the two massive river and lough catchments to the north and south, the Erne and the Shannon. It holds no pike, but there are char, perch, minnows, and sticklebacks. It is about 10,000 acres in extent, only moderate in size by Irish standards, and we might reasonably expect all the indigenous trout to mingle, either at random or by accident, and to interbreed. Yet here the scientists tell us, and the fishermen can see with their own eyes, that there are four quite distinct types of native trout, racially pure since the last of the ancient ice sheet retreated, which the scientists have declared to be sufficiently different in their genetic make-up and isolated in their reproductive behaviour to be classed as four separate species. What a gem of a lough, to have retained these ancient forms of trout in such pure form; and a powerful argument for conserving its waters, free of man-made pollution, free of the genetic contamination that might occur if alien strains of trout were ever to be released into it, and free of the survival pressures that might arise if alien predators such as pike were to arrive and gain a foothold.

Another ancient fish of these glaciated depths is the Arctic char, a cousin of the trout and the salmon, and bearing the tiny rounded adipose fin that is the badge of all the salmonid species. It tends to live in big shoals that seldom come to the surface, and only the occasional char ever falls to the fisherman's fly. It is easiest to see these char not in the flesh but as tiny pixels on a sonar display screen, typically at depths of between forty and eighty feet, and sometimes in such numbers that the fish-finder screen appears to be indicating a snow-storm. But troll a tiny flickering lure of twinkling gold deep down, and you may be rewarded by the distant tugging take of a char. In the net, it looks like a delicate flake of silver, with other subtle hues of iridescent green and rosy-purple. Its weight is unlikely to exceed eight or ten ounces at most, and a char weighing over a pound is a trophy indeed. Especially when spawning time approaches, the males have a striking livery of greens and golden reds, and another definitive char feature is apparent, the pale creamy forward edges of their pectoral, ventral and caudal fins. (Anglers on stillwater fisheries that have been stocked with what are commonly referred to as American brook trout will be able to use the same diagnostic features to tell that the brookie is, in fact, a member of the char family.)

The char's delicacy of appearance is matched by its flesh, which is still prized by a few enthusiasts, but which was much more widely appreciated in Victorian and Edwardian days. The English Lakes, especially Windermere, had a flourishing commercial char fishing industry to supply the eager demand, and potted char was especially popular both as a culinary technique and as a method of preserving fish which might otherwise not keep for long. The little hand-painted char pots are now valuable collectors' pieces in their own right. There are still a few traditional char fishers in Cumbria, who troll deep in the old way, sometimes with tiny hand-fashioned spoon-baits of pure silver and gold. But Lough Melvin, like most of the deep char lakes of Ireland and Scotland, seems never to have sustained any commercial char fishing, although at Lough Eske, another glacial trench just twenty miles to the north and nestling in the southern folds of the Bluestack Mountains, there is a long tradition among the local people of netting the char when they shoal in the shallows in November before spawning.

All the salmonids require water of great purity, and therefore represent a useful barometer of the cleanliness of the freshwater environment. When acidification and its invariable acompaniment, the deposition of aluminium and other toxic metals, strike a freshwater catchment, the char will be the first victims, with grayling, trout and salmon also suffering if the pollution continues. The same goes for enrichment caused by slurry run-off or silage seepage, both serious threats to the purity of the water that salmonids require. There are increasingly stiff penalties for negligent farmers who allow slurry or silage effluent to enter watercourses, and fish-kills from these causes are becoming less frequent. But acidification remains a hovering threat for many fisheries in the north and west of the British Isles, especially where the headwaters of river and loch catchments are ploughed and planted with commercially-grown conifers.

The vast new commercial forests are composed of trees which tend to acidify their environment directly, as well as indirectly, by capturing and holding acidic rain and then releasing it suddenly and with the addition of trace metals such as aluminium, to flush quickly down newly-dug drainage systems and into the rivers and lochs. The soil and the underlying rock has no time to exercise a buffering or de-acidifying influence, as happens when water seeps slowly; and where the existing soils are already highly acidic, as with blanket peat overlying rock such as granite, the delicate balance may be pushed too far towards unacceptably high acidity. Some of the hill lochs of Galloway are now gin-clear and totally fishless as a consequence of acidification following afforestation. Small wonder, therefore, that environmentalists and fishermen bite their lips apprehensively when another swathe of hill land goes under the forester's plough. It is a cruel prospect to envisage wild fish of immemorially ancient genetic uniqueness being rendered extinct in just a few years, if ill-planned forestry should cause the the precarious balance of water purity to veer towards an insupportable degree of acidity.

Elsewhere in Britain the char's fortunes have swung in the other direction. In the west Highlands of Scotland there are numerous deep char lochs, and some of these have recently been chosen by commercial fish-farmers as sites for floating fish cages. The captive fish are fed on highly nutritious pelleted foods, and a proportion of this feed simply drops down through the cages' meshes and into the free waters of the lochs. The wild trout, and the char, have come to know of this new source of excellent food, and regularly cruise in the vicinity of the cages to pick up the stray feed pellets. The result has been some almost incredible growth rates among populations of char that formerly averaged no more than ten or twelve ounces. Rod-and-line anglers from the late 1970s onwards began to catch bigger and bigger char, until the specimen fish committee eventually decided to suspend the records for the species. Middle-aged Arctic char of up to seven and eight pounds have been caught in Scotland since the mid-1980s, and many of these have been released to live on and grow still bigger. It now seems a virtual certainty that a British char of ten pounds or more will be caught before the 1990s are out, and it will almost certainly be taken by an angler trolling in the vicinity of fish cages on a Highland loch. Fish of this size are something quite new to the British fishery scene, having previously only been encountered among the much larger races of migratory char of North America.

The Watcher and the Roe

Roe are special, in my case for at least two reasons. For anyone who grew up in the United Kingdom in the post-war years, Bambi, the archetypal deer of childhood, was undoubtedly a roe, even if Walt Disney actually had in mind a White-tail or some other North American species. In elegance and elfin charm the roe is the quintessence of Bambi, and that alone makes it special. Childhood impressions run deep and are lasting.

And then there was the almost exotic unfamiliarity of roe for a boy growing up in Ireland, where these deer do not exist. As the ice-sheet retreated about 11,000 years ago, the land bridge between Ireland and the rest of Europe was breached by the rising sea before roe could colonise that far west, and so Ireland was left with only the red deer and the giant Irish deer (often wrongly called an elk) as indigenous species. The vast *megaloceros giganteus* became extinct — wags say the twelve-feet spread of its antlers caused it to get stuck among the trees of the ancient Irish forests. The Anglo-Normans introduced fallow deer to their deer parks as a ready source of meat on the hoof; and Victorian acclimatisers brought the Asiatic sika deer and released them in their Irish demesnes. But still there were no roe.

In late medieval and modern times the roe's former British status as a worthy beast of venery had sunk very low, a trend which began when Edward III revised the Forest Laws in the 1340s and demoted the roe from the nobility of a beast of the chase to the comparative lowliness of a beast of warren, a status no higher than the rabbit. There was never much British interest in the roe as a quarry for hounds, although a few short-lived packs of roebuck hounds were established, and the typical British hunting man's opinion of the roe was one of indifference at best, and often of hostility, since young and undisciplined hounds were liable to leave the trail of the intended fox or hare and riot on the scent of roe in coverts. All very different from the attitude of the French with their passion for *la chasse au chevreuil*, esteemed by connoisseurs as *la plus fine*, the most refined and sophisticated of all their ritualised forms of *la chasse à courre*. By the time organised game shooting and Highland red deer stalking had evolved in mid-Victorian times roe in Britain had sunk to the level of vermin, snared and shotgunned at random, and persecuted in all their British haunts by landowners, foresters, gamekeepers and farmers.

Only a handful of British enthusiasts studied their ways. J. G. Millais, the painter and sportsman, Frank Wallace, the mysterious 'Snaffle', A.E. Gathorne-Hardy and Henry Tegner were pioneer champions of British roe, and their efforts led eventually to the introduction of proper statutory safeguards and protection for roe in the Deer Act of 1963. Redeemed at last from misunderstanding and cruel persecution, roe began to take their place as a respected mammal. Yet, almost incredibly, in the 1990s there are still landowners who flout the law and carry out roe drives, beating out the coverts and driving roe to lines of standing shotgunners, who shoot every roe seen, regardless of age or sex and with complete disregard for the close seasons. The cull is haphazard, and wounding is commonplace. This loveliest of British native deer deserves better than that.

In nineteenth century Ireland a few landowners toyed with the idea of introducing roe, but only one actually did so. In the 1860s the Gore-Booth family brought roe from Dupplin Castle in Perthshire to their Irish estate at Lissadell in Co. Sligo, on Ireland's north-western coast. There, in lush woods and grassland over rich limestone the deer flourished beyond the wildest expectations. All deer colonising new areas tend to do well, producing high body weights and strong antler growth. But these roe, taken from the acidic, calcium-deficient conditions of Perthshire to the rich limestone land of north Connaught responded with a surge of spectacular antler growth that remains unparalleled in Europe.

Conventional six-point roe heads at Lissadell were magnificent in size, weight and symmetry, and some displayed a riot of profuse growth with many additional points. The amazing Lissadell 12-pointer stole the show at the 1912 exhibition of British deer heads organised in London by *Country Life* magazine. It had been found dead at Lissadell, apparently killed in a fight with another buck, and Sir Henry Gore-Booth reckoned that it was only about the third largest that the estate had produced. The others have not survived, and we can only imagine what they may have been like. But the 12-pointer's massive craggy shape can still be seen, hanging in the billiard room of that four-square house built of grey Sligo limestone, where the poet William Butler Yeats had stayed and unsuccessfully wooed the two beautiful Gore-Booth daughters, Constance and Eva. This is the most remarkable surviving memento of Ireland's only roe, which flourished so spectacularly before the entire population was shot to extinction in the 1930s, to make way for a new afforestation scheme. Today there are no roe in Ireland.

Unknown in the countryside of my childhood, roe therefore assumed the special attraction of novelty when I spent early holidays in Britain and Europe, and later when I lived for spells in the Highlands, where there were not only red deer on the hills but also roe in the birch woods, and in the wooded straths and glens. By 1982 new work had taken me to southern England, where I lived in a pretty village among the chalk downland and broadleafed woodlands of Wessex, where the borders of Wiltshire, Hampshire and Dorset converge. There, on the ancient Cranborne Chase, live some of the finest roe in Europe, and for almost six years I watched and studied and photographed and stalked them in much of my spare time, eagerly making up for the lost years. There followed yet more opportunities to see and pursue roe, in the Breckland woods of East Anglia, in the great commercial softwood forests of the north of England and the Scottish Borders, and in the Highlands.

Wild deer live on the edge of human vision, even for those who know them well and study them with the benefit of experience. Deer in parks and zoos have a bovine tameness that gives no hint of the alertness and shrinking shyness of their wild cousins, that live among the shadows and in the dappled depths of woods, that emerge silently and materialise without apparent movement in the blinking of an eye as you wait and watch by a woodland edge at dusk.

Usually so timid and retiring, roe can sometimes be surprisingly bold and inquisitive, and noisily vocal, too. A whiff of scent, the hated scent of men or dogs, sends them fleeing, bouncing away in horror through the trees and undergrowth. Those moist, shiny jet-black noses are ultra-sensitive receptors of the slightest message carried on the breeze. Those large, independently-mobile ears continually flick and twist to catch any sounds that might betoken danger, wonderful natural listening devices of which man-made directional discs are only a crude approximation. Roe's eyesight, too, is quick to pick up sudden movements, but it is strangely limited in its ability to resolve static objects, especially if they are not silhouetted but blend in against a similarly coloured background. Even an unmoving human outline on a skyline may fail to spell danger with anything like the urgency of a moving person.

But stand, preferably in sombre clothes and with the pallor of your face shaded by a hat's brim, against a background of trees or lower vegetation, and a roe may simply not notice you at all, if the breeze is in your favour. It may graze up to within a few yards, a few feet, so close you would expect it to take fright at the hammering vibrations of your thumping heartbeat. Move your arms with slow, smooth deliberation to raise your binoculars with gloved hands and the deer may still remain undisturbed. But do so abruptly and show the pale flash of your uncovered hands, and heads will whip upright, bodies will stiffen on the alert, and most deer will whirl around and rush off in sudden alarm.

But roe — at least some roe — may not. Some innate disposition, inquisitiveness perhaps, can make them hesitate, or cause them to make an initial bolting dash and then pause and look back at you. Their heads tilt upwards, nostrils flare, and a fleshy pale pink tongue flicks outwards and upwards repeatedly to moisten that black nose, to heighten still further its sensitivity to air-borne particles of scent. Necks extend upwards, and those direction-finding ears twist independently in search of the least give-away sound. A slim foreleg is raised and held poised aloft, questioning and attentive. It may be lowered and raised again, or, more typically, the roe may change feet, raising the other foreleg, or advancing with a staccato stiffness and a gentle stamping action, like a high-pacing horse in a succession of freeze-frames. So eager to solve the puzzle of this unidentified shape, the roe may weave its head right and left in an effort to resolve the indistinct and tantalising image.

And then it barks. Close by, it is an abrupt and explosive *baw*, gruff and hoarse and sharp. At a distance it is more mellow, yet still with a curt, terrier-like timbre of gruffness and petulance. In some localities roe are surprisingly noisy, and there are times when they behave more vocally than usual, for reasons we can sometimes only guess at. Equally puzzling are the times and places when roe simply don't bark.

The barking of roe has an echoing quality, especially when it is heard at a distance among high, mature trees; and the lie of the land can accentuate this. Some bits of roe country have particular acoustic characteristics that enhance and heighten the resonant sounds of their barking. In particular, two Scottish glens have shown me this year after year, where roe wander among wooded slopes that rise above the banks of rivers, one a large and sweeping salmon river, the other a smaller tumbling stream. In both places there is a reverberating echo, often the case near water, where sounds ring among the rocks and trees in a way that may stimulate the deer to bark more often and for longer than they would otherwise. Whatever the reason, the roe in both places are continually noisy to a degree that is unknown in many other places that are home to just as many deer, but where barking is very seldom heard.

In some localities I have found that the roe behave as if they are actually dumb. One of these is a quiet corner of Wessex, a varied expanse of broadleaved woodland and open downland and arable farmland where the roe population is high. It has been one of my favourite roe-watching haunts for years, thanks to the kindness of friends who indulge my interest, and of farmers, who tolerate the deer and like to see them about the fields, but also like them to yield an occasional dividend in the form of venison for their freezers, or a cheque from the game dealer, in exchange for their depredations on crops.

Over a period of eleven years I have spent hundreds, and probably thousands, of hours sitting watching for deer there, or stalking them on foot, at all kinds of hours and at every season of the year. I have watched them feeding, and fighting, and bucks chasing does in the rut — and I have never once heard any of them utter a vocal sound of any kind. Even when alarmed suddenly, they never bark. I have lost count of the number of times I have startled a roe, or a family of roe, by accident, perhaps when I have been stalking in the woods or creeping furtively along a hedgerow with my eyes on other deer at a distance. The roe love to lie up in the hedgerows on warm days, and that is often when I suddenly stumble upon them — almost literally, sometimes — by chance, when I am working my way along a hedgerow to get a closer look at an animal feeding out in the neighbouring field.

Suddenly there is a scrambling, scrabbling upheaval and a brief thumping of hooves as a deer jumps to its feet and bolts out of the hedge, usually heading full tilt out across one of the wide fields. Some will simply flee until they are lost to sight, while others will dash perhaps eighty or a hundred yards and then stop stock-still to look back at the intruder. And they never make any vocal sound. In the woods, others will detect my presence by scent, and then all I hear is the brushing, scampering sound of deer making off by pushing through thick undergrowth or long maize. Again, no barking. Yet here at home, near the Scottish border, when a deer hidden in a thick plantation of young spruce winds me or hears my approach, it will bark in alarm more often than not, and its husky, resonant, repeated calls, half bark, half cough, will mark its departure as it makes off, usually downwind, in a series of typical dashes and brief halts.

Roe dislike sheep, at least here in the border country of fenced and hedged grass parks that tend to be well stocked with sheep from April to October, and elsewhere on low ground where sheep densities are high. They will very rarely graze in a field with sheep, and often continue to shun a grassy pasture for weeks after the sheep have been taken off elsewhere, presumably because the ground is still tainted with the lingering scent of sheep. Yet they are often to be seen browsing or grazing contentedly just the other side of a fence or hedgerow only a few yards away from sheep. On the heathery hills of parts of the Southern Uplands and in the Highlands many roe live their lives largely in the open, almost like miniature red deer, but there sheep are stocked only at very low densities, and close encounters between the two animals are infrequent. By contrast, roe and cattle seem to be able to coexist quite happily on high ground and low.

Here in east Dumfriesshire the roe are usually only to be seen out in the open fields in winter, when much of the pastureland is left empty after the stock have been taken away to their in-wintering quarters. But in spring and summer they are hidden away in the woods, colonising small shelter belts of spruce and larch as well as the larger commercial plantations, and often occurring in the mature mixed species woodlands that are chiefly used as pheasant holding coverts. There is enough feeding for them to attain good body weights, but the bucks' antler growth is often meagre and spindly, the results of a deficiency of the calcium and minerals that produces such superb antlers on richer land like the chalk downs of Wessex and Sussex.

A lot has been said and written about the advisability of culling roe selectively, sparing the best heads and encouraging them to remain and pass on their genes to future generations. In fact, such a management policy is highly questionable where the calcium and mineral content of the animals' natural forage is on the poor side. As long ago as the 1870s those little Perthshire roe that were transplanted to the limestone pastures of Lissadell showed what amazing things optimum feeding can do for antler development, and the same lesson is continually underlined across many acidic areas of Britain. Every now and then a young buck, whose first or second head would normally be little more than two spindly spikes, will find his way daily during the winter months, when his shed antlers are regrowing, to mineral licks and troughs of cattle cake, and the result may be a magnificent pair of antlers that would score silver or even gold medal points on the international CIC assessment. Deprive the same buck of such rich feeding during the following winter, and the result is likely to be a reversion to the light, thin antlers typical of all the other local roe. The correlation between antler weight and feeding is direct, and only when feeding is optimal can roe deer managers hope to improve things still further by selective culling of the less fine examples.

Much more important for effective roe management in Scotland and many other parts of Britain is the need to take account of the animals' ages and social organisation, and adjust the cull so as to keep damage to agriculture and forestry to a minimum. A mature roebuck is a strongly territorial creature, who will unhesitatingly keep other, younger bucks out of his home range, which may comprise quite a large area. A wise manager will see that senior buck as an asset, and will concentrate on cropping the younger bucks and the very old. But let a trophy hunter shoot that resident buck, whose head may be the most impressive in the area, and the consequence may be an influx of the younger bucks that the old boy had been holding at bay. They each proceed to take up smaller individual territories, and the result may be a sudden and sometimes spectacular upsurge of fraying and browsing damage to trees, shrubs and crops, and an understandably angry landowner or forester. That is when the guns may be ordered in, and an unnecessary and avoidable shoot-out attempted, far too high a price to pay for the privilege of having the senior buck's head hanging on the trophy hunter's wall. This very drama was enacted on a wooded estate just a few miles from my home, reinforcing the need for thoughtfully-applied roe management strategies if damage and panic measures are to be avoided.

Where roe are not continually harassed, and have sufficient peace to establish rhythms of individual and social activity, they are particularly rewarding deer to study. These are not herd animals, and generally live in small family groups in Britain, although the roe of central and northern Europe often form temporary herds of up to sixty animals as a response to the severe cold and restricted feeding of the mid-winter months. In a typical instance in southern Scotland, a family party of roe may take up residence in a small plantation of twenty or thirty acres of mixed woodland or commercial conifers, the group perhaps consisting of a middle-aged buck and doe, one or two young fawns (kids, strictly speaking) born the previous May, and a yearling, often a doe born the spring before.

Their movements tend to fall into regular patterns of resting and lying up in the cover of the trees by day, followed by movement out into the clearing and rides towards dusk, and sometimes into adjacent fields and open ground to feed by night. First light finds them beginning to graze back towards the woods again, and eventually to another day's secretive rest. Often the movements of undisturbed individual deer can be chronometer-like in their timing, allowing us to predict almost to the minute when a particular animal will cross a woodland ride at a certain point, or move through an accustomed gap. This is a particularly useful trait when we take a visitor out to watch deer, allowing us to place the watcher at the best spot at the right time and tell them where and when to expect to see a roe show itself.

Different groups have their individual routines. One family I watched lived in a large shelter belt of woods on a dairy farm, where the workers came out to gather the cows for milking very early in the morning, returning the beasts to the fields an hour or so later, after which there would usually be no more human activity until late afternoon. There the roe would slip back into cover early, just before the men and their cattle dogs arrived, and would move out again after the cows had returned and the men had gone away. Often they stayed out in the fields until mid-morning or later, unless some unscheduled passer-by caused them to dash back to the cover of the trees.

In mid-winter the woods can be achingly cold places, and a hard overnight frost followed by a morning of bright winter sunshine will often tempt the roe out into the open, to revel in the warmth of the sun on their backs for an hour or two, before they slip back and are lost to view.

The even tenor of their ways may have a quiet predictability for much of the year, but the unexpected may happen when the rut comes around in late July and early August. The roe rut, and the rutting time of most woodland deer, has none of the roaring, blustering *braggadocio* of red deer on the open Highland hills in autumn, when the corries and glens come alive to the belling challenges of stags that gather and herd their hind harems in a continual frenzy of noise and activity. But roe nevertheless become vocal and active in ways that are quite uncharacteristic of the rest of the year. The accustomed rhythms of resting, movement and feeding are abandoned for a week or two, and mature bucks and sexually receptive does can be found on the move at any time of the day.

Mid-morning and late afternoon are perhaps the main periods in which to expect to see rutting roe on the move, often in the form of wild chasings as a buck pursues a doe in season. This may appear to be a coy female trying to evade the attentions of an over-ardent suitor, until you realise the extent to which the doe may really be egging on the buck. More than once I have seen a chasing buck collapse, his pink tongue frothing and his foxy-red flanks heaving with exertion and exhaustion in the warm air of a summer's day, only to see the fleeing doe turn back to him and strike him with her forefeet, urging him to get to his feet again. And despite their usual aversion to mingling with sheep, I have often seen a pair of chasing roe hurtling repeatedly around a field full of ewes and well-grown lambs, that continued to graze and doze in total unconcern at the dashings and circlings that went on at full tilt among them.

In addition to the gruff barking sounds that roe may make at any time of the year, the rut is also a time of reedy, piping calls, subtle and plaintive sounds that maintain contact

between the deer in the dense and lush undergrowth of late summer, when visibility in the woods is at is poorest. The doe in season will almost always have her twin kids to care for and suckle, dappled little Bambis that were born just eight or nine weeks earlier, and that lie up in motionless and almost scentless concealment until the doe returns to them. The kids have their contact calls to their mother, including a high and anguished bleat of alarm that may bring the doe instantly to the rescue at full gallop, and the doe in season has a soft and plangent call to signal her presence to the buck.

Roe watchers and stalkers in Europe have made careful studies of these calls and their effects on the deer, and there is a long tradition in northern and central Europe of imitating the calls of roe. The original method, still used by some purists, is the *blatt*, a blade of grass or a strip of tree leaf held in tension between the joints of both thumbs and blown upon to make it vibrate like the reed in a woodwind instrument, simulating the high-pitched cry of a deer. The same method is a well-established ploy among British gamekeepers and poachers, to "squeak up" a fox or a hare or a rabbit, but its application to roe is something that was unknown in Britain until it was imported by roe enthusiasts who had seen roe-calling in action in Europe. The post-war enthusiasm for roe deer in Britain, as fascinating mammals to study and as worthy quarry for the stalker, has been steadily assisted by many techniques and a great deal of expertise derived from continental Europe, and the art of calling roe is perhaps the most skilful and delicate of all.

The rustic simplicity of the *blatt* has been largely replaced by a variety of purpose-made roe calls and home-made variations of them, and a small wind orchestra of instruments is now available to those who want to try their hand at this subtle art. It is a skill best learned by the side of a master, or perhaps from an audio cassette, and when it works the results can be startlingly impressive. Three or four plaintive bleating calls blown from the concealment of an observation platform or a high seat should be followed by silent watchfulness. Anything may happen. A buck may come galloping at full tilt in almost instant response, or perhaps a doe bringing a buck close behind her. Or many minutes may pass before a trim red shape slips into view, moving gently towards the call with infinite care. The masters of roe-calling, the hunters and foresters of Europe, can modulate their calls to play upon the deers' responses with astonishing subtlety and skill, bringing a roe almost to within arm's reach, then allowing it to drift away, then recalling it to your feet again and again. They can lure roe with the certainty of a Pied Piper, casting a seemingly magical spell on these most elusive and wary of animals. To witness a skilled roe-caller at work is to glimpse an uncanny degree of sensitive rapport between a man and a wild creature.

A few *peep*-ing sounds from a roe-call may attract an individual animal at almost any time of the year, but a positive response can never be assured, even for an expert, and the time of the calling is limited to the brief period of the summer rut, after which the roe resume their more usual patterns of their quiet lives. The only significant exception to this may occur in October, when, as many roe watchers believe, a brief secondary or 'false' rut may take place, a fleeting resurgence of sexual activity that is still a matter of controversy among roe experts. One explanation is that any autumn rut may involve deer that failed to mate during the summer.

A River through the Year

The river means different things to different people. To most of the fishermen it really seems not to exist outside the months from April to October, when the first of the spring trouting begins and last of the salmon fishing ends. After that, few of them walk its banks until spring comes again. To the farmers it is both an ally and a threat — an ever-present natural drinking trough for cattle and sheep, a watery boundary to their fields that saves having to put up a fence, but also a continual nibbler-away at their land, overflowing and undermining the banks on the outsides of the bends when the big floods come churning down. To the wanton fly-tippers it is a handy place to dump old cars, mattresses and builders' rubble by night, while a few careless agricultural contractors use it for casual disposal of fertiliser bags and the black plastic sheeting that wraps silage bales. After a high flood the ugly jetsam festoons the branches of trees eight feet and more above the normal water level, hanging like black funereal tassels.

The river is the parish boundary, its course the march line that denotes the extent of many farms. It flows westwards from high sheepwalks and the fringes of hill forestry plantations into a gradually softening landscape of meadows and a few arable fields. A handful of stone bridges span it at intervals, and one in particular marks the point where it changes quite abruptly in character from a bubbling hill stream to a gentler lowland river. I call it the dipper bridge, or sometimes the kingfisher bridge, because I have never seen a dipper downstream of it, nor a kingfisher above it. Upstream it bubbles and rushes down a steepish gradient, twisting and curling through miniature gorges and along streamy stretches of broken water, the natural haunts of dippers. Below, the current slows and becomes a succession of smooth glides, slipping with silent ease between low fields. Kingfishers wait with the silent watchfulness of sentinels, then flash into action in a blurred streak of electric blue when they make a smash-and-grab attack on some small fish, usually a small trout or a salmon parr.

Below one of the lowest pools there is an old eel-weir, the stout remains of a once-handsome piece of Victorian engineering. Once or twice in late autumn and winter it is still used for its original purpose, usually on the darkest moonless nights when the eels are on the move downstream, impelled by their ancient magnetic attraction to the sea, and the long spawning run south-westwards towards the Sargasso. They haul them out in traps and nets that have not changed in design since these men's great-grandfathers enacted the same ritual, taking their twisting, writhing harvest from the dark water. They find big brown trout in their hauls, too, bigger than anyone with a fishing rod ever seems to encounter here. Fish of six and even seven pounds, fish as big as grilse but with none of their silvery grace. These are mature resident trout, chunky and heavily muscled, in all the imposing colours of their end-of-year spawning livery, and heavy with eggs or milt. Rough, calloused, careful hands slip them back into the watery darkness, to breed more generations of big fish to haunt fishermen's close-season dreams.

The salmon spawn further up, well above the dipper bridge. We find their redds each winter near the junction pool, where a tributary flows in from the north. The water spreads out across a wide, shallow delta of good spawning gravel, a tumbled bed of rounded chunks of sandstone and basalt the size of billiard balls. From a hillock above the junction we can sit and look down on the redds, polaroid glasses enabling our eyes to cut through the reflections and opening up a clear subsurface view of the mating salmon. The pairs of fish are aligned in echelon, the female in front, twisting and heaving to excavate the gravel with her tail and the powerful water pressure that her writhing movements generate. The cock fish waits astern, only moving forward to shed his milt onto her eggs after the redd is complete. Often there are little male salmon parr hanging around the redds too, occasionally slipping alongside the egg-laying female and quickly shedding their tiny store of milt onto the eggs before the protective and aggressive adult cock lunges at them and drives them away. These little pre-migratory males can successfully fertilise an adult female's eggs: it is Nature's insurance policy, just in case there should ever be a shortage of mature cock salmon to pair with the hens.

The junction pool is also a regular haunt of cormorants. We often see their black cruciform shapes from the road as we drive by, as they perch on one of three large midstream rocks, ragged wings oustretched to dry. They look like refugees from a fire, blackened and singed. We are miles from the sea, their roosting caves and their nesting cliffs, but these are opportunist feeders, and there are plenty of fry and parr and smolts in these upstream shallows. Tom the river-keeper tells how he used to pot them from the road, poking a rifle from his Land Rover window in the days before they were put on the protected list — 'but there would always be another one there in its place on the rocks the next week. There must have been a cormorants' waiting list for the privilege of fishing the junction pool!' Today the riparian owners and fishery proprietors have to apply for a special licence to cull cormorants and goosanders if predation on fish is excessive; and the police tend to disapprove of anyone pointing a rifle out of a vehicle window!

Tom's grandfather was river-keeper on this stretch in the 1880s, and he potted more than cormorants. Then, there was a simplistic belief that everything that was not game was bound to be a threat to it in some way. The landowners insisted on it, and the keepers' jobs depended on a display of victims, as proof that they were doing their work conscientiously. And so dippers and kingfishers, and even the sandpipers that flute in spring along the stony margins of the river, all figured on the vermin gibbet. Only their most exotic feathers were saved, and given to the retired ghillie who tied flies for the visiting fishermen. So little birds innocent of any serious predation on game fish furnished in death bright feathers for flies that would capture trout and salmon — a wry irony.

Most of the river's length is populated by duck; mallard throughout the year, with a sprinkling of teal from late summer onwards, and occasional influxes of pochard, tufted duck, wigeon and shoveler in winter, when storms along the coast drive them inland. On windy nights they appear out of the dusky gloom, rocketing in with the gales behind them, turning and setting their wings into the wind, dipping with lowered feet like paddles and silhouetted against the last light in the sky, then suddenly lost to sight as they drop below the fringe of dark conifers that line the river, where they splash-land noisily but unseen. If the gale has blown itself out by morning they will usually have gone again, back to the salt marshes and merses. The teal come and go throughout the autumn and early winter, zipping low up the river, intent on reaching some little pool up in the hills, or dabbling and twirling in some of the calmer small backwaters and river pools. When surprised, they rocket up from the water almost vertically, heading slightly into the wind and only levelling out when they have breasted the tops of the trees, to make a tight turn and swing off downwind like little darts on flickering wings.

The resident mallard are more phlegmatic, usually preferring to swim away well ahead of any approaching intruder, and take wing with more reluctance and a splashy noisiness, as they rise and climb at almost forty-five degrees to clear the fringing larches and spruces. By Christmas in most years their small flocks have begun to break up, and many are already living and moving about in pairs before the turn of the year. By early February the pairs will have staked their claims to their chosen stretches of river, each pair with an average of about three-quarters of a mile of stream. They are more conspicuous along the river in February and March than their neighbours, the goosanders, which tend to be less active about the open pools and slow glides. Instead they skulk among the rocks or tucked in close under the grassy banks much of the time, and we pass them by unawares unless one of the dogs gets a whiff of scent and plunges in to dislodge them. Then they are startlingly obvious, with white wing markings flashing brightly as they rise and bank and circle, usually swinging out over the fields and climbing higher as they go, turning back overhead to take a good look at us, before they turn away and follow the line of the river, flying just level with the tops of the trees with skimming wingbeats that are shallow like the ducks', yet clearly slower and more purposefully powerful.

From late February onwards, in mild years, there are signs of activity in the quiet backwaters of the river, in the little pools of floodwater left over from the highest winter spates, and on ponds close to the river. The annual invasions of toads and frogs get underway, usually accompanied by the gentle and continuous sounds of croakings and slight splashings among the reeds and the fringes of rushes and sedges. Of the two ponds near the house, linked by a little feeder stream, one is preferred by the toads and the other is the frogs' favourite.

Toad spawn appears quite quickly in the upper pond, looking like long glassy ropes of jet seed-pearls. On the lower one, just eighty yards away, clear water suddenly gives way to a mass of gelatinous frogspawn, like a glutinous slobber of opaque porridge, or some form of rice pudding studded with tiny black raisins.

Herons and mallard annually invade the two little ponds to feast on both lots of spawn. The duck will drag the glistening ropes of toad spawn out of the water and leave uneaten lengths discarded and stranded on the grassy banks. They gorge and linger, and each year it looks at though they intend to stay and nest on the upper pond, but after a couple of weeks they are gone again, perhaps deterred by the proximity of the drive and the occasional but inevitable comings and goings of cars just a few yards from the water's edge. The lower pond, though more quietly situated, never seems to hold any attractions for nesting duck, perhaps because twin electricity cables cross just above it and constitute a hazard to aerial navigation. I have often noticed that such overhead wires and cables can prevent wildfowl from using well-fed flight ponds, even in hard winters when the ample supplies of fresh food put out there must represent a powerful attraction.

By late April the goosanders on the river are at their most furtive, before the young hatch and are led by their mothers down from their nest holes in tree stumps and rocky niches well above the water, to paddle and slip off downstream, or to linger among the streamy runs and eddies. The young goosanders are defensive and quick to hide, slipping adroitly under the cover of bankside vegetation and into clumps of reeds when danger looms, while both the parent birds are alert and eager to distract attention from

their young. A typical strategy is for the female to make brief splashy rushes across the water, like a wounded bird trying to escape, and this is an almost irresistible invitation for all but the steadiest dog to dive in and try to grab her, while the male flies low and steadily up and down, skimming just feet above the water, and making occasional wide sweeps out aross the open fields, keeping so low that the clumps of reeds almost sway in the slipstream of his wings, and tempting our gaze, and the dogs' dashings, away from the river and the hiding places of the young.

There is a scattering of goosander nests among the streams and hill drains that form the headwaters, where the young birds are hatched in holes and forks of old bankside trees, or in cavities among the rocks and sandy soil of the high banks. The lower reaches of the river receive a steady influx of goosanders and their young in late spring, as mothers and their broods of small chicks come bobbing and tripping down on the current, dropping gradually downstream over a period of several weeks as the chicks grow and fledge on the richer feeding of the pools and glides.

Further down still, beyond the confluence of the tributary stream and the main course of the river, late May brings the annual sight of the salmon and sea trout smolts' migration. These flickering little bars of silver began life high in the headwaters three years earlier, when the spawning adults splashed and wallowed in the shallows to excavate redds in the gravel and lay their eggs as the short days of late autumn darkened into the depths of winter. By the following May, after their gravelly resting places had been pummelled and sluiced by the great rolling floods and spates of winter, the eggs had hatched and the little alevins had begun independent lives in the nursery streams, subsisting first on their yolk-sacs, their natural food reserves after hatching, and then on the insect and invertebrate life of the little burns.

Then come the parr markings, the oval blotches like evenly-spaced dark fingerprints on their flanks, against a background of shiny yellows and silvers and olives and greens, flecked with tiny speckles of dark brown and red. These parr fling themselves with zest onto the troutfisher's flies, eagerly engulfing the fake offering of feathers and tinsels and wools with an indiscriminate delight, so different from the wary adult trout that are the fishers' quarry. We release them gently, and none flickers away back into the depths of the pools without taking with it a silent expression of goodwill, in hopes that it may flourish and that we may meet again when their adulthood has made fish and fisherman more evenly matched. The sea trout parr will eventually smoltify too, and slip downstream to the waiting waters of the Solway Firth, and there will thrive and grow heavy on the rich offshore feeding in the Irish Sea. The little salmon have an altogether more daunting odyssey ahead of them, a long migration out through the North Channel and across the waters of the North Atlantic, to the rich high seas feeding grounds off Greenland, from which they will depart to face more dangers and hundreds of miles of return migration before they re-enter the river of their birth as lithe and heavily-muscled mature salmon, or as elegant little grilse that have spent only one winter away at sea.

First they undergo a transformation in the river, their hormonal balances shifting and producing a secretion of guanine that turns their blotched and speckled flanks a shimmering silver. In this bright livery they become smolts, adapted by the natural progression of their development to face the harsh transition from fresh to salt water. It has taken almost three years for them to grow steadily from an egg to this six-inch stage weighing barely three ounces; another twelve months will see a surge of size and weight to over twenty inches and as much as five or six pounds, and those that nose their way back up the Solway after two or three winters at sea may weigh twenty pounds and more, the stuff of salmon fishers' fondest dreams. The Solway rivers have a good mixture of mature salmon and young grilse, like most Scottish rivers, and there seems to be some correlation between the age of the little smolt when it goes to sea and the length of time it will spend there. Many three-year-old smolts from Scottish and Irish rivers will be back as grilse in a year, while in the richer alkaline waters of southern rivers like the Hampshire Avon a salmon may grow fast, smoltify, and leave the river after only one year of life, to spend perhaps three winters at sea, not returning until it is a massive twenty-five or thirty pounds.

On the warm days of May and early June we often see the shoals of smolts splashing and leaping in the pools and the riffles, full of energy and a seeming expectancy, almost a carnival atmosphere, as they rise and pluck at almost every passing insect and piece of floating debris. The parties of little silver migrants drop steadily down the river and are lost to sight, and their going coincides with the appearance of the first of the early summer grilse, the returnees that left as smolts last spring and are now back again in their ancestral river, beautifully neat-headed and with flanks of opalescent silver, the annual miracles of the river and the sea.

In the river one of the minor hazards that parr and smolts and mature salmon alike have to face is the otter. Happily, here in the Scottish Borders and among the rivers of neighbouring Cumbria and Northumberland the otter is still quite a common mammal, and may even be gradually increasing. Even when British otter populations reached their nadir in the 1960s and 1970s, these northern rivers of the hill country still sustained a fair number of otters, their waters remaining free of the worst exploitation and pollution that meant the end of otters on thousands of miles of rivers further to the south. Here, perhaps their chief problem has been competition with feral mink, which are now firmly established in every river catchment from Cornwall to Sutherland. These most unwelcome additions to Britain's wild mammals have done incalculable damage to the ecology of rivers and the wildlife that lives along their banks, and the self-styled animal lovers who released mink from captivity have actually been guilty of one of the worst crimes against British wildlife in recent times. About the only good thing to be said about mink is that they are relatively easy to trap, and good river-keeping by bailiffs and riparian owners can usually keep on top of the problem fairly readily. But it is highly unlikely that we shall ever be rid of feral mink altogether, and shall probably have to learn to live with them — at low numbers, I hope.

To see a mink, or fresh signs of mink, by the river is guaranteed to send us home in a bad frame of mind, just as surely as a glimpse of an otter is sure to make it a red letter day. Finest of all was a glorious half-hour in April when we stood and watched two otters as they dived and swam and played and groomed together in a river pool just twenty yards away from us. I had a compact camera in my jacket pocket, and snapped away for a full thirty-six exposures until the mechanism clunked and began to make rewinding noises. No spare film to carry on shooting, but there were bound to be at least a few goodish shots in the bag, or so I thought, until I opened the camera back at the house — to find it was quite empty. I still have nightmares about those otter pictures that might have been.

Tarka the otter, and his creator Henry Williamson, deserve places of honour in any hall of fame for fictional creatures and those who gave them life, in print or on film. For Tarka has the integrity of a real otter, and makes no unfair or cynical demands on his readers' emotions. He is a wild and mysteriously captivating creature, from his birth in the riverbank holt to his last gasp in the book's final and powerful pages. He is no sanitised soft toy for the nursery, no cute Hollywood representation of a furry mammal that invites cuddling or tugs at our heartstrings with the blatantly anthropomorphic charm of Lassie the Wonderdog. Williamson's wild Devon otter was, and remains, an elusive free spirit, as wild as the waters he swims in, as much a predator of trout and salmon, and as much a quarry for hounds and huntsmen, as he was over half a century ago, and as otters have been since the first ancient naturalists wrote about them.

The age-old sport of otter hunting has come to an end now, the wise and voluntary decision of the otter hunters themselves, who saw a respected quarry becoming rare in the 1960s in the face of pollution and development, its haunts despoiled by human activity and human filth, or repopulated by feral mink, exotic and destructive escapees from fur farms. There was a time when every countryman's hand was against them, even gentle Izaak Walton, the contemplative man whose recreation was fishing and who declared himself 'therefore an enemy to the otter, he does me and my friends so much mischief; for you are to know that we anglers all love one another: and therefore do I hate the otter perfectly, even for their sakes that are of my brotherhood'. But otters thrived despite centuries of hunting and trapping by sportsmen and river keepers, and by commercial trappers whose prize was the otter's thick, rich pelt. Then pollution and drainage and development did what direct human persecution had always failed to do, and drove the otter to the edge of extinction over much of southern Britain.

Now the future of the otter lies in the ability of individual landowners, industrial and agricultural managers, the National Rivers Authority, and conservationists to work together, to give Britain's remaining otters an environment that is fit for them to live in. Already there are encouraging signs, as otter numbers steadily recover in England's eastern counties and in Williamson's West Country. North of the border and across the Irish Sea they remain well established, while the seaweedy lochs and voes of the Hebrides, Orkney and Shetland still regularly echo to the sound of the otters' whistles and chitterings.

And otters still hunt and eat trout and salmon, too. But today's game fishers are more tolerant than their forefathers, and coexist happily with otters. Most anglers are only too pleased to catch a glimpse of one, a moment of delight in what may be long hours of dogged and unrewarded fishing. In the shining river valleys of the West Country and Wales otters are a familiar sight to those who go night fishing for sea trout, while in Scotland and Ireland it is not uncommon for trout and salmon fishers to see otters about and active in broad daylight in the rivers, the estuaries, and even among the rocks and wrack of the sea shore. They grumble occasionally, as fishermen always will, about the risk of an otter panicking the fish in a pool and making them less likely to come to the fly. But every flyfisher has to have some excuse, some plausible alibi for coming home with an empty creel — and an otter is as good as scapegoat as any. He is always a joy to see, and we owe him at least the deference due to a professional fisherman from us fumbling amateurs.

Most of the amateurs are game fishers, eager for salmon and trout, who cast the first lines of the new season in mid-February. There are still a few early spring salmon that come nosing back up the river, and these may be some of the biggest of the year, but they are scarcer each year, and highly prized. The sea trout and grilse begin to return in May and June, and the main salmon run comes in late September and October, with fresh fish still entering the river in November and early December, long after the salmon rods have been hung up for another winter, alongside the trout rods that went into storage at the end of September.

But a few enthusiasts keep their trouting rods set up and in action for a while longer, not for the trout and sea trout that are now on the spawning redds, but for another member of the salmon family, the grayling. Elegant, silvery, and delicate, it has the little adipose fin that is the badge of all the salmonid tribe, but it also has a massive, sail-like, rayed dorsal fin, the forked tail and the large scales that we tend to associate with the cyprinids, the so-called coarse fish, and it shares their habit of spawning in the spring, when the trout and salmon are back in season once again. This hybrid quality has led to the grayling's traditional exclusion from the prized inner circle of the true game fish, which is absurd for a species that is magnificently sporting, and also makes superb and delicate eating. (Its Latin name, *Thymallus thymallus*, perpetuates the long-held belief that a freshly-caught grayling is supposed to have a scent like thyme, which I confess I have never been able to detect in any of the grayling that I have caught, sniffed and eaten.) It is also the most fastidious of all river fish, susceptible to the slightest degree of pollution, and its presence is therefore a welcome indicator that the water quality is excellent.

A summer grayling can be a poor thing, lean and weak and spent after its recent spawning compared with the high-season vigour of trout and sea trout. But it comes into its own as the leaves begin to turn, having recovered condition on the rich feeding of summer. As the days grow colder and the hours of daylight lessen, the amount of

obvious fly life on the river decreases. The myriad hatches of summer are gone for another year, and the natural world is slipping into winter somnolence. But all but the very coldest days of late autumn and winter may enjoy a brief hour or two, usually in early afternoon, when the temperature rises just enough to allow a slight resumption of insect hatching. These are the times the grayling flyfisher prizes, the precious hours when you can cast a subsurface nymph or a tiny floating dry fly to tempt a feeding grayling.

I have one or two favourite spots for watching grayling; useful vantage points on top of steep banks where I can look down into deep pools and steady glides, and where the miracle of polarised lenses allows me to see beneath the surface reflections to where the grayling are lying, like dark torpedoes. An old English name for the grayling is the umber, probably derived from *ombre*, the French for 'shadow', though perhaps also a reference to the reddish hue of the mature fish's large dorsal fin. I prefer to think of them as watery shadows, elusive and sometimes almost opaque shapes in the stream. Even when you know what to look for, it can take a few moments before you make them out clearly. Often their presence is first betrayed by a brief flash of creamy white beneath the surface as a grayling opens its mouth to feed, and that momentary flicker of white can be just enough to help focus our attention on a resting, feeding group of fish.

The spiritual homes of expert British grayling fishers are the spring-fed chalk streams of southern England, and the rivers of northern England like the Dove, the Wharfe and the Wye, and all the Yorkshire rivers. There grayling have been studied, and tactics and flies have been developed by grayling gurus like Pritt and Walbran, Righyni and Sawyer, to an extent that is the equal of even the finest grayling areas of Austria or Scandinavia. But on the Scottish side of the border we have grayling, too, and the Grayling Society has its keen Scottish adherents, who are glad of the opportunity to extend their flyfishing season to Christmas and sometimes beyond in search of grayling, awaiting that brief window of wan warmth that triggers off a slight hatch and brings grayling up to a fly.

A Year of Wings

Does anyone nowadays play the association game? Beloved of early psychoanalysts, and then adopted as a parlour game, it can be amusing — and revealing — to see what word springs to mind when prompted by another. When you say 'skylarks' I will reply 'rifle-ranges'. What might an imaginative psychologist conclude? A childhood trauma involving the shooting of a bird, perhaps, or some vague theory of natural beauty threatened by man-made violence? The reality is much simpler and less sinister.

My boyhood summers, and many summer days since, were taken up with target rifle shooting, as an alternative to school cricket, at which I was inept, and which also entailed long miserable afternoons wheezing and sniffling and sneezing in the annual wretchedness of hay fever. On the open turf of a rifle range at over 1,000 feet there were always cool, largely pollen-free breezes, a sport I was good at — and there were skylarks.

As they soared and reeled and sang high overhead we snuggled our cheeks against the aromatically oiled wood of rifle stocks and sent our shots whizzing and cracking across the rough grasses and heather with as much care as we could, longing to see the spurt of sand at the other end, for the target to dip and the marking frame to come up in its place to announce that we had actually succeeded in hitting that dinnerplate-sized bullseye 500 yards away. Our real target was a coveted place on the school team that would go to Bisley in July. The skylarks' endless tumbling songs were the steady continuo punctuated all afternoon by the crackle of shots, the clinking of ejected brass cartridge cases, and the erratic ringing of the ancient field telephones that gave us a tenuous link with the target butts.

Bird watching became a regular pastime while we waited between shooting details. We had telescopes for spotting the shots, old brass-tubed leftovers from the first world war and Home Guard observation duties, with unbloomed lenses, murky optics, and a nominal magnification of about 20x. Dull weather reduced their images to sombre grey, like peering through smog or dirty cotton wool, while warmth and brightness made them dance and shimmer in the magnified heat haze, with an added kaleidoscopic sparkle of splintered points of light. They worked their best when the light was bright and the air cool, and then we could see every detail of the skylarks' feathering, and the raised tufts of their crests when they descended and perched on the short grass of the short-distance firing points between us or the targets. Shot after shot screamed over them as they hopped and rested and sunbathed and simply stood calmly, serene and unruffled by the sonic cracks of the high-velocity slugs of cupro-nickel that swept just inches above them.

There were meadow pipits, too, that rose from the grasses and dipped again, less eyecatching than the crested larks. And there were wheatears, erect and plump and bright on turf hummocks and occasional jutting rocks. They were pert and smart, especially the handsome cock with his livery of pale grey back, black wings and tail-tip, and subtle pastel yellow, with the distinctive white tail and rump that shows well when he is at rest, and flashes unmistakably when he flies. This is an insect-eater, an annual spring returnee from the winter warmth of Africa, that frequents open countryside, and especially likes the fringes of moorland and grassy upland sheepwalks. Like the curlew, he returns as one of the surest signs that a new spring has arrived.

The wheatear is a relation of the ortolan, that traditional delight of European gourmets, especially in southern France, where the cooking and eating of ortolans is attended by solemn ritual, the diners covering their heads with large linen napkins to catch and hold every breath of the unique aroma and bouquet and funnel it in undiluted richness to the appreciative nostrils of the gourmet, just as friars' balsam is directed to the nose and lungs of an ague sufferer.

Wheatears nest in crevices and depressions in the ground, and are especially inclined to make use of rabbit scrapes and burrows for breeding. These birds abounded on the rabbit-riddled chalk downlands of Wessex and Sussex in pre-myxomatosis times, and especially in the middle of the last century, when they were trapped in their tens of thousands in horsehair snares and limed traps for the commercial poulterers of London's Leadenhall market, and thence to the cafes and restaurants of Paris and the rest of France. In Norfolk the wheatear's local name is 'coney-chuck', which nicely combines a representation of the bird's sharp clicking call with the fact that it often uses coneys' burrows both for nesting and as boltholes in which to shelter when danger threatens.

How the name wheatear arose is less obvious. Francis Willughby, the eminent ornithologist of the 1670s, wrote that in Sussex its name refers to 'the time of wheat harvest, [when] they wax very fat', presumably, he thought, from gorging on an excess of ears of wheat. John Taylor, the poet and a slightly older contemporary of Willughby, devoted an entire poem in 1654 to the delights of eating roasted wheatears, and maintained that they were so called 'because they come when wheat is yearly reaped'. This must surely be a mistake, or at least an error of observation, since wheatears arrive in spring, heralding the planting of the spring-sown crops of those days, and not their harvesting four or five months later. And as for eating wheat, this little bird is actually an insectivore, like the swallows and martins that return northwards with them, which occasionally adds a few small worms and small snails to its diet. When seen among growing cereals or on post-harvest stubbles it is not in search of grain but of invertebrate and insect material. In Northampton it is known by the unflattering name of 'clodhopper', surely more commonly applied to a clumsy, heavy individual than to something as alert and nimble as this. But it accurately records how the wheatear will forage for insects, larvae and worms among the ridges and furrows of freshly- ploughed land in the spring.

Local vernacular names tend to emphasis the bird's prominent white rump, which is one of the most conspicuous markings on any small British bird, and also the sharp abruptness of its call. In Cornwall it is the 'White Ass' or 'Whittol' — i.e. 'white tail', while in central and eastern English counties it is the 'White Rump' or the 'White Tail'; and to those with a canny ear for its call it is variously the 'Check Bird', the 'Chock', the 'Chuck', the 'Chack' and the 'Chat'. Other onomatopoeic names are the 'Horse Snatch' and the 'Horse Musher', which imply a comparison of the wheatear's clicking call and the distinctive clicking noises used by waggoners and ploughmen to urge on their horses.

In the Southern Uplands of Scotland, and the nearby hills of Cumbria and Northumberland, the curlews and the wheatears are among the earliest birds to make a conspicuous and audible return in spring. I should hate to live far from the springtime calls of curlews. The lapwings follow soon after, and the oyster-catchers too; and the occasional osprey appears also, following the river courses on their northward

movements towards the Highlands and their nesting places. They are fond of stopping off at fish farms and stocked trout ponds, which must be their equivalent of motorway cafes or the *relais des routiers* that refresh long-distance drivers. High priority legal protection ensures their free passage, and few trout-breeders will begrudge them a fish or two in passing. Occasionally one becomes entangled in the nets that are spread to protect stew-ponds from the depredations of the resident herons, and the threshings of a large and well-taloned raptor can make it almost hopelessly ensnared, until careful (and heavily gauntletted) hands disentangle its trammels and allow it to go on its way.

Easter is a moveable feast and despite its annual shifts of date, it still makes a handy seasonal milestone to denote April and the main onset of spring. The first swallows return to this part of Dumfriesshire around mid-April, first as an occasional vanguard bird and then in numbers within a week or ten days. The martins come next, and the swifts last of the three. By early May the wren that builds her nest in the stables will have slipped away with her young, leaving the rafters and the ventilation gaps free for the bigger, busy, noisy migrants to take possession. Their 'pendant beds and procreant cradles' are a great deal more welcome than the starlings'. These annexe the disused chimney of the woodshed from March onwards, rearing successive clutches of young, and making their all-too-evident mark in doing so. They fly to and fro across the front of the house, carrying away the youngsters' faecal sacs in their bills, and dropping these and their own contributions across the parked cars, as if it were a bombing range. By May the starlings' flightpath to and from their nest looks as though the area has been pelted with hundreds of miniature flour-bombs.

Perhaps the highlights of the spring, and certainly the latest to arrive and settle, are the flycatchers. The pied ones come first, anytime from late May onwards, and the crisply monochrome cock bird immediately assumes his favourite lookout position on the electricity wires that are strung above the back lawn, from the old sycamores to the corner of the house. Is it the same individual, or does a son learn from his father? We need a ringer to fit some coloured rings to old and young, so we can tell which it is in future years. The pied flycatchers lose no time in nesting, by which time we invariably see the arrival of the last of all, the spotted flycatchers.

Less striking in plumage, these are more conspicuous in behaviour, perhaps because their invariable breeding territory is so readily seen from the kitchen windows. Their nest site has not changed for six seasons, a niche tight against the wall where a heavy old down-pipe and an intersecting offshoot make a right-angle. Victorian exterior plumbing may not look too good, but it has its bonuses, and the mossy cup of the flycatchers' nest is securely tucked in the sheltered hollow between the pipes and the masonry. On that north-facing wall it never receives direct sunlight, and the temperature must remain more constant there than elsewhere on the other walls.

The adults have two accustomed perching places, one on the top of a garden gate, the other a few yards away on the crosspiece of what used to be an archway into an old vegetable garden, both quite a bit lower than the pied flycatchers' preferred perches. This used to give concern when we had a particularly predatory cat, but he seemed more content with the easier pickings to be had by raiding songbirds' nests in the field hedges, after which he would proudly lay out the spoils on the front doorstep for us to admire. To compound the enormity of this daily carnage, his vociferous mewings for tinned food confirmed that he had no intention of eating the day's bag, evidently preferring processed kangaroo-meat or whatever it was, so we bade him an unregretful farewell as he was taken off to a new and more useful life, controlling an epidemic of mice at a farm in Invernesshire. He has not found his way back yet, which suits us and our birds; and his replacements, two feline sisters of uncertain but somewhat oriental breeding, are no threat to the bird population, since they show a singleminded devotion to the abundant local field voles as their prey, which the older labrador will steal and crunch up with relish if they are unwise enough to leave them to be admired.

The pied flycatchers seem to prefer hunting their insects in and around the older trees, which make a bower of shadows in the corner of the garden. The spotted flycatchers have different tactics, perching on their two usual hawking places and making repeated forays among the clouds of little insects that fill the warm air under the young apple trees and the larger shrubs. Their agility and hovering ability makes them appear as though they are occasionally trying to imitate the sky-dancing of a hunting kestrel. When the young have fledged and flown the corner of the garden visible from the kitchen can sometimes seem to be full of flitting, twisting shapes as they perch and dash and hover and weave.

By May the high hills are at their best for the best of all spring expeditions, a visit to the hill burns after trout, taking in a peregrine eyrie or two en route. The trout of the hills take time to recover their full condition and fitness after spawning, and are not usually at their best before early May. In the acidic burns the feeding is limited in quality and quantity, and that is reflected in the average weights and size of the fish. Few attain more than half a pound at their peak, and six ounces is a more typical moorland fish — a nice breakfast size, especially if taken on light tackle, with a tiny dry fly cast upstream and grabbed in a swirling slash as its tumbles back on the peaty water that slides and foams like dark beer. This is Lilliputian flyfishing, the rod a mere seven feet, the line no heavier than the backing line we use for salmon fishing, and the fine nylon cast a gossamer filament that would make Izaak Walton's horsehair look like a hawser.

For hill trouting I avoid the streams that are fed by the new networks of hill drains. These are too erratically spatey in character now, too prone to pelting tumults of flood water that quickly dry up into tiny rivulets once the rain has passed. Instead I — and the trout — prefer the burns that have a steady seepage of water from peat, where the extremes of droughts and rainstorms are mitigated by the buffering of self-draining topsoils and natural run-off. Here there are always deep pools and steady glides, with cool holes under the banks where fish can flee from the bright sun, and a riverine environment where trout can establish feeding territories and grow as steadily as the food supplies will allow.

The hills are a hungry place, where protein is at a premium, and not only for the fish. The round-leaved sundew is a plant of the damp acidic moorlands, superbly adapted for harvesting protein in the form of insects. It is not unknown for me to sink down on one knee in preparation for popping a fly over a likely trout lie, only to feel a seeping of chilly water through my breeks and find that I am sinking knee-first into a sphagnum flush; and often its convoluted surface of pale yellowish-greens can be seen to be studded with the reddish leaves of the sundew. Sphagnum is *the* acidic plant, its moss saturated with many times its own weight of water, and also an excellent naturally sterile wound dressing that was sent in quantities to the western front in the first world war. The sundew cohabits happily in what would otherwise be this barren environment by spreading its traps for the unwary, its attractive red leaves that draw insects to it, and its glistening glandular hairs that add to the fatal visual attraction, only to hold the settling insect in

a sticky and ineluctable grasp where its struggles merely ensure it is held more firmly, and then begin the gradual processes by which the captive expires, dissolves and is absorbed, leaving only the indigestible fragments of mouth-parts and wing-cases. Nothing is wasted. Richard Jefferies and Gerard Manley Hopkins had got it wrong when they wrote of 'nature all in a rush with richness' and the 'progidality of nature' Here there is nothing prodigal about the way life is sustained and itself sustains other life, no superfluity in the enactment of the physical laws governing the conservation of energy.

These high streams are mostly above the dipper line, for the water ouzel prefers the lower reaches between the high moors and the valleys. Instead there is a scattering of grey wagtails and sandpipers along the burns' courses; and on both the heathery slopes that lead up to each of the nesting crags that the peregrines use there is always a pair of ring ouzels. These 'mountain blackbirds' are among the easiest of all upland birds to describe to anyone unfamiliar with the fauna of the hills, for the cock is just the same size and build and colour as the common blackbird of farmland and suburbia, with the notable addition of a bright white gorget that blazes like a silver crescent. Like the white on the breast of the dipper, the 'water ouzel', this can be seen clearly at some distance, especially as these birds are fond of perching prominently on rocks and suchlike places where they can be seen easily. The female, like the hen blackbird, has not the matt sable body colour of her mate, but is a soft, deep brown, with a crescent of pale throat feathers that is more muted than the vivid monochrome contrasts of the male.

I have occasionally found the remains of adult ring ouzels in peregrine eyries, but never at sites where the ouzels had a nesting place close by. Peregrines, and other hawks too, seem to enter into a kind of neighbourly pact not to prey on other birds that nest in the immediate vicinity of their eyries, and I have often found ring ouzels nesting happily very close to both peregrines and merlins. They return to the high hills quite early in the year, and I have frequently found ouzels in mid-March, when my 'peregrinations' begin around St Patrick's Day, the cock birds' clear ringing calls carrying long distances on the upland breezes. By late May in years of good spring weather it is not unusual to see the barely-fledged young of the first brood fluttering about under the supervision of the cock ouzel while the female is sitting tight and getting on with the serious business of incubating her second clutch of eggs.

When I was watching nesting peregrines fairly seriously and continuously in the late 1960s and early 1970s as part of a breeding survey, the British Trust for Ornithology was also in the process of amassing data for its magnificent Atlas of British breeding species.

My peregrinations took me into the spring and summer haunts of various other breeding birds that were not my prime objective, and it was a good opportunity to make notes on what I saw on my expeditions, especially as regards the less common upland and mountain birds. Ring ouzels were one of these, and I was able to gather a good deal of data about nesting pairs on my peregrine eyrie visits. Often the clearest giveaway to indicate breeding success was the sight of an adult ouzel returning to its well concealed nest with a billful of food for the young, and this was evidence enough to enter a definite 'FY' note on the recording card. Sometimes, if I actually had enough time and luck to find the nest and see the young ouzels, I was even able to enter a triumphant 'NY', and later on there might be clear sightings of the scruffy-looking fledged young, which meant it was time to note down the final clincher, 'FlY'.

By early July the frenzied and often vocal activity of nesting, on high ground and low, has given way to the comparative calm and quiet of high summer. Another season's young have fledged, the young peregrines in their juvenile plumage of browns and buffs hang around the general vicinity of their eyrie site, and the noises of territorial claims, courtship, aggression and eager food calls have been replaced by a time of quiet, as the fledged young get on with the serious business of growing and the adults are moulting. It is not a lively time in the hills, although the weather is more reliable than usual, and we sometimes have to set out early if we are to use the dogs for the pre-shoot grouse counts, before the warmth of the sun burns off the dew and the last of the scent. On a sunny morning it may be too warm for the dogs to work well after ten o'clock, when the moors become dry and scentless and dusty with pollen from the flowering heather, and overheated pointers and setters are chiefly interested in finding a sphagnum pool or a cool boghole to wallow in.

Summer is a hiatus in the changing seasons, a period when everything seems to mark time for a while compared with the succession of changes that have overcome the landscape and its wildlife since the winter solstice and the turn of the year. At home, the garden and the nearby woods are quieter than they have been for months, and along the

river the dippers are less vocal than at any other time of the year. The rookery is silent and deserted now, and the principal birdsong is the steady cooing of woodpigeons from their favourite perches among the larches. There is an occasional soft mewing from the young sparrowhawks that were hatched there in May, and still hang around their home wood.

The birdlife around the house begins to show the first signs of renewed restlessness and change in September, with the last broods of swallows and martins fledged and beginning to drift away. As the summer visitors from the Mediterranean and Africa gradually slip away, I find it is worth watching the European weather map for some indications of when the first autumn arrivals from Scandinavia and northern Europe can be expected. The timing of their coming depends quite a lot on the weather in their northern summering grounds, with the early onset of cold autumn weather invariably pushing them south sooner than usual.

More local weather affects bird movements too, and if there are storms and early frosts on the hills the teal and snipe will come down to the lower marshes and ponds sooner than normal. By the first week of September the rushy inland marshes will have a sprinkling of snipe, probably resident birds that have made their short migration down from the moors, but the period of the full moon in late September and October is the traditional time to expect the first influxes of the wintering migrant snipe from Iceland, Scandinavia and the Baltic. It is a further three weeks or so before they are followed by their less common cousins, the jack snipe, that breed in Russia and up towards the Arctic.

The scolding scream of a jay is one of the most familiar bird sounds of mixed and broadleafed woodlands throughout the British Isles, yet for every ten birds that we hear we are unlikely to glimpse more than one or two. Exhibitionists both by their calls and their behaviour, jays nevertheless have a remarkable capacity for staying just out of sight. In the full foliage of late summer no woodland bird is easy to see, and jays are as elusive as any.

But I always tend to associate jays and their squalling cries with the thinning woodland canopy of autumn and with the bare copses and plantations of mid-winter. A scattering of oaks and beeches among the other tree species nearly always guarantees the presence of jays, especially when there are acorns and beech mast for them to feed on, and there has been a succession of good mast years in the Dumfriesshire woodlands. The bill of the jay looks stout and workmanlike, as do those of all the crow tribe, but the plump oval of an acorn seems as though the jay's bill had been tailor-made to grip it. With the keen eyes

common to all corvids, jays seem able to spot their favourite nuts with little or none of the scufflings and leaf-tossing searchings that other birds use to locate them. They will drop suddenly from high in the trees to pounce on an acorn or a cluster of beech nuts, pause for a moment with that bill a-gape and grasping the food, then off on broad and rounded wings without more delay.

By late October the family parties of jays have begun to break up, but a local abundance of food may still concentrate the birds in the woods where fruiting beech and oak predominate. By the New Year they are more scattered, but each little copse and plantation still seems to hold its pair, taking the last of the winter's wild foods and benefitting too from the supplementary feeding put out for the pheasants. Silhouetted against the sky, their shapes are simply dark against the customary greyness of a winter sky, but in the hand they reveal a remarkable subtlety of colouring, from hues of warm mushroom and muted cinnamon on the head and neck, to the dazzling electric blue of those exotic dark-barred wing flashes, shimmering with the brightest lapis lazuli that ever haunted the fondest dreams of a miniaturist or an illuminator of manuscripts.

The jays and other omnivorous birds of the woodlands and fields, and the squirrels too, get first pick of the autumn nuts and wild fruits, but by late October they will have been joined by wintering competitors for many of the same foods, the fieldfares and waxwings that arrive in flickering flocks from the north. The first sight I get of them is usually from my study window, as a party sweeps in over the house and alights on the two flat fields that lead away to the stone-walled boundary and the rising hilly fields beyond, or stop and perch restlessly in the almost bare branches of a rounded beech tree that marks the far edge of the garden. The scattered windfalls in orchards are always a draw for the birds, which find them bruised and soggy but still full of fruit among the strewn leaves. The blood-berried rowans of the valley fringes, that have been bent with the weight of fruit since early August, quickly begin to lose them to the invaders' eager appetites. Hips and haws and holly berries likewise begin to disappear, but always a good deal later into the winter, after the most luscious of the birds' preferred foods have been eaten first.

Fieldfares are usually the first northern migrants we see around the house, when they arrive in flickering, shifting flocks that move restlessly from field to field and from one belt of trees to another. They are streamlined, trim birds, with an alert manner, and their arrival always seems to coincide with an increase in the numbers of sparrowhawks we see locally. Occasionally we glimpse a flock scattering in panic as a sparrowhawk rushes among them and tries to grab one, and the little male — the 'musket' in falconers' parlance — seems to be by far the more successful in taking fieldfares. Nimble and fiery, they dash and swerve and snatch in a blur of speed. I sometimes wonder if sparrowhawks and other raptors follow the northern migrants southwards, or if this seasonal increase in sparrowhawk activity is simply the work of our resident birds, including those mewing branchers that seemed so inept just a couple of months earlier. Some old sporting and cookery books say that fieldfares were once a great delicacy; the sparrowhawks evidently concur.

By early October the resident breeding plover from the hills have come down to the low pastures and the marshes for the winter, where they are joined by tens of thousands of others that come in from the north, mainly from Iceland. Their wheeling flocks congregate along the margins of the Solway Firth, especially near the estuaries of the Esk and the Eden, where there is a fringe of rich grassland along the shore. There they feed in the moist soils, or stand motionless in flocks, all heads into the wind, one leg tucked up beneath them, and stirring only occasionally, when one stretches its wings out sideways, first one side, then the other, or 'warbles' with both wings upstretched and almost meeting above its back, giving a distinctive flash of silvery white from its pale axillary feathering. 'A stand of plover' is an excellent collective term for a resting flock, and so too is 'a wing of plover' for the birds in flight. The singular noun is definitive, for although there may actually be a thousand flickering wings, the flock moves and turns and manoeuvres as a disciplined single unit, hundreds of individuals moving in unison like a single organism controlled by just one nervous system, a miracle of formation flying and aerial mastery.

The last and largest of the autumn arrivals, and the real signs that winter is coming, are the wild geese. High echelons of greylags and pinkfeet pass over the house, barking and honking and chattering to each other as they go, steadily set on a southwest course for the Solway Firth just a few miles away. Their numbers build up steadily from late October and reach their peak in November. On most of the big estates the birds are protected, finding ad hoc sanctuaries there that help to offset the shooting pressure they face on the foreshore.

It is easy to be sentimental about geese, but one incident made me ponder more than any other. One evening in late December - it was midwinter's night, in fact — I slipped out of the house to fetch a briefcase I had left in the car. It was mild and very misty. I took the case from the car and had my hand on the doorknob ready to go back indoors when I heard the clear, wild calling of a goose, somewhere in the foggy gloom overhead. It called, and seemed to circle and call again and again, just one solitary greylag. On and on it called and circled, the focal point of its movements being a short distance to the east of the house, just over the fields towards the little church. Probably a bird that had been separated in the fog from the rest of the flock, perhaps an adult bird whose mate had been shot earlier that day and which was searching vainly for it.

But something more made my spine tingle. It was 21 December 1990, and almost twenty past seven in the evening — two years to the minute since the cockpit of a Pan Am jumbo jet had crashed onto those fields just beyond the house. Flight 103, the *Maid of*

the Seas, had exploded six miles up, killing 259 passengers and crew in the air, and eleven people in Lockerbie, and propelling the quiet Borders town and the parish of Tundergarth into a grim international limelight. A book of names of the dead lies open in the little chapel of remembrance in the churchyard; and now the disembodied, invisible presence of a wild goose circled and called above it in the mist, a lonely sound that seemed to call for a response that never came. For almost twenty minutes it cried and flew steadily around, then fell silent and was gone into the foggy darkness of the longest night of the year.